The Overcomers

RICHARD WURMBRAND

Bridge-Logos

Orlando, Florida 32822

Bridge-Logos
Orlando, Florida 32822 USA

The Overcomers
by Richard Wurmbrand

Copyright © 2006 by Bridge-Logos

Library of Congress Catalog Card Number: 2006925621
International Standard Book Number: 0-88270-206-8

Unless otherwise identified, all Scripture quotations and names are taken from the King James Version of the Bible unless otherwise indicated.

G1.318x.FB.m606.35250

TABLE OF CONTENTS

RICHARD WURMBRAND

PREFACE

HE PURPOSE OF THIS BOOK IS TO PRESENT A SERIES of *overcomers*—men and women who not only endured for the sake of their faith, but used obstacles to ascend to great spiritual heights.

When Jesus entered Jerusalem riding on a colt the crowd chanted to Him, "Hosanna in the highest" (Mark 11:10). *Hosanna* is a contraction of two Hebrew words: *Hosha,* "save," and *na,* "please." Therefore, "Hosanna in the highest" means, "Please save us in the highest sense of this word," or, "Save us on the highest plane."

I can save a hungry orphan from his hunger by giving a little money for his support. I can save him even better by contributing regularly to his bodily needs. But I can save him best by adopting him and making him heir of all I possess.

Individuals asked and obtained from Jesus different kinds of salvation: from sickness, from immediate trouble, from sins, from death. But He can provide a salvation much higher than all of these: He can save us from being *only* human. He can give beyond anything we might dare to ask or think. He offers us the privilege of one day sitting with Him and His Father on His throne, from which universes are created and ruled (see Revelation 3:21).

Those called to such heights soar even now above average men and women, even if outwardly they are lowly or downtrodden.

I was in jail with a remarkable man, Pastor Francis Vishky, leader of the organization *Christian Endeavor* in Romania. He was sentenced to twenty-two years because of sermons that displeased the Communists. His wife and seven children were deported to a desert place, where it was difficult to obtain bread and water. His heavenly calm even in such a situation was amazing. It was the calm of a heavenly throne.

I would like to tell you what happened at the moment of his arrest. On that particular morning the whole family was at the breakfast table, where they read Psalm 23:4-5: "Yea, though I walk through the valley of the shadow of death, I will fear no evil: for thou art with me; thy rod and thy staff they comfort me. Thou preparest a table before me in the presence of mine enemies: thou anointest my head with oil, my cup runneth over."

Without knocking, three officers of the Secret Police broke into the house. "This is a search," they said, with no further explanation. But everyone knew that after the search the father would be taken to prison. The family continued to eat quietly. The police wondered that they still had an appetite and remained calm.

Vishky later said that they understood the Psalm better under those tense circumstances than they had previously. God had not promised that His children would *not* pass through the valley of the shadow of death, but that in it they would fear no evil.

"He prepares a table before us in the presence of our enemies." On the table we will not always have what we desire. He can serve us with suffering, trials, deportation, jail, even violent death. But the valley through which we pass is called the valley of the *shadow* of death, not of death. The shadow of a dog cannot bite—the shadow of death cannot kill.

Vishky added, "The Jews were commanded to eat the whole Passover lamb—with its head, legs, and entrails" (Exodus 12:9). The entrails were far from appetizing and there was not much meat on the legs. We have to accept the whole Jesus. Not only what is pleasant to us, but also His crown of thorns.

RICHARD WURMBRAND

In jail, Vishky maintained the same calm, the same serenity. This happens when one knows he is destined for a throne. Not only crowned kings but also crowned princes have to behave royally. We learn how to obtain such a character from those at this high level of faith. That is why in this book I will provide many examples of faith under pressure.

Perhaps some might say that I have given "too many examples." But how much time do we spend watching television, listening to radio, and reading newspapers and magazines? A poll taken in the United States reveals that only 9% of those who speak to us in the media have a connection with religion of any kind. But by continual repetition they fill the needs of the 80% of American churchgoers with the thoughts of people with no high ideals and little concern for God—or even of immoral people who cannot possibly help us live a righteous life.

The Bible is repetitious. It deals with 1,300 persons. Some of them are luminous examples of faith, others are average believers. To know their names and something about their lives is extremely useful, just as it was useful to me to have certain contacts when I first came to the United States. Many of these Bible characters will be our friends in heaven. Others show by their ugly lives what kind of people we should be wary of if we wish to enter heaven ourselves. So it is good for you to get acquainted with the heroes of faith I describe.

Since Jesus' ascension to heaven, there have been many who continue in His footsteps. These "fill up in their flesh what is lacking in the afflictions of Christ" (Colossians 1:24). These will be the main subject of this book.

This Book Will Profit You

Thousands of books appear each year. Why should you read this one? How will you profit from it? Should a person read unprofitable books as well? Must we not be as choosy in reading books as we are in selecting the food we eat?

The wrong kind of book can poison a life. Marx, Nietzsche, Lenin, Hitler, Mao, de Sade and many more wrote books that others read, believe, and act upon. Tens of millions of people have died as a result in wars and revolutions. De Sade wrote books that inflamed the mind to violence and lust. Books can be dangerous. Some have taught men to hate and despise their fellow men, with the result that they hated and were hated. Mankind would be much better off if some books had never been written.

The Bible says that for fear of the authorities who had just crucified Jesus, His first disciples were assembled behind closed doors (John 20:19). It was wise to do so. They too were in danger of being arrested and killed. But if it is wise to keep the doors shut for fear of persecutors who can kill only the body, should we not also keep the gates of the mind shut so that no pernicious ideas, no false images of reality, no lies can enter and destroy the soul?

Evagre of Pantus, a third-century Greek church teacher, wrote "Be the door-keeper of your heart and don't let thoughts enter it without interrogating them first: 'On whose side are you, on mine or on my adversary's?'" Readers should ask themselves before starting a book, *"How can this book profit me? I have a short life and a very limited time for reading. Why should I spend it on this particular book? What is its importance for me?"*

Many have a prejudice against religion. They argue, "It speaks about lofty things without practical usefulness in this world." I once thought like this and was surprised therefore to find what a tremendous role the subject of "profit" plays in the Bible.

The Communists tried to build an economy on something other than the desire for profit and failed. God himself placed it within the human heart. The Bible warns against "vanity, and things wherein there is no profit" (Jeremiah 16:19). It teaches men to calculate "what profit he has from all his labor (Ecclesiastes 1:3). It claims, "Godliness is profitable unto all things, having promise of the life that now is, and of that which is to come" (1 Timothy 4:8). It puts the question, "What profit is it that we have kept God's ordinance?" (Malachi 3:14).

The apostle Paul did exactly what I do at this moment. He wrote, "I speak for your own profit" (1 Corinthians 7:35). Jesus himself taught explicitly that we should seek what is profitable. He said, "What is a man profited, if he shall gain the whole world and lose his own soul?" (Matthew 16:26).

My claim is that this book will profit you.

PART 1

NO GREATER LOVE

1

THE STORY OF THE ROTHSCHILD DYNASTY

WHEN I SPEAK TO THE JEWS ABOUT CHRIST, I often illustrate the significance of what he has done for us by telling them the story of how the Rothschild dynasty of multi-millionaires began. Its founder, Mayer Amshel Rothschild, had been a poor boy who served in the house of Rabbi David Moshe of Chortkov. This rabbi had set aside in a drawer 200 golden coins as a dowry for his daughter. Rothschild married a girl from another town, where he opened a little shop that did quite well. Years passed, and the time came for the rabbi's daughter to marry. As the wedding approached, the rabbi opened the drawer to take out the coins to give to the bridegroom, only to discover to his horror that the money was not there. No one in the house had any explanation as to how it could have disappeared. The suspicion fell on Rothschild. They asked themselves: Where did he get the money to open his shop? Surely he was the thief.

The rabbi defended him: "It is not right to accuse anyone without proof."

But the family insisted, "You must go and speak to him. Otherwise we will be disgraced. The guests have started to arrive, and the wedding will not take place."

Reluctantly the rabbi went, apologized for having to ask such an embarrassing question, but explained the terrible predicament in which he found himself. Looking his former employee in the eye he asked, "Do you know something about the money?"

Rothschild was silent a few minutes, then said, "I have stolen it. I will repay it here and now. Please forgive me."

The rabbi, who had an understanding for human sin, gladly forgave him. The wedding took place, and he officiated with great joy. Rothschild went broke. Many years later it was discovered that the 200 gold coins had been stolen by a servant girl, who shared it with a lover. At a drunken party the lover bragged how he came to possess the money. He was arrested, and both acknowledged their theft. The rabbi went to Rothschild and asked him pointedly, "Why did you confess to a sin you had not committed? And why did you give me the money?"

He replied, "I saw you terribly sad. I imagined the weeping of your wife and of the girl. I was ready to give you all my money immediately to make up for the loss, but I knew you would not accept such a sacrifice from me. So I had to say it was your money, which I stole. So you were peaceful and had joy."

Then Rabbi David Moshe blessed him: "May God reward this deed of yours by giving you and all your descendants great riches." The blessing was fulfilled. The Rothschilds are among the richest men in the world. One can only admire such a deed. But should we stop at admiration, or should we strive to become heroes ourselves in some area of life?

This Rothschild's deed has the fragrance of our inspiration from Jesus. To make His message and gift more acceptable to us, Jesus took the lowliest appearance of a man, allowing Himself to be born not only into a poor family but in a humble stable for beasts. Even more, He became sin for us and ended His earthly life crucified among thieves. He went so far as to declare that our sins are His.

~2~

THE ONLY FEMALE MONK

WHEN I SPEAK IN A CHRISTIAN ORTHODOX church, I tell the story of Theodora from their *Lives of Saints*, which—sadly—the average Orthodox never reads.

When Theodora's mother died, her father decided to become a monk and suggested that she enter a convent. But she was so attached to her father that she decided to go to the monastery with him. Since she was not conspicuously feminine in appearance, she was accepted as a monk. Because of her—or more appropriately to her disguise, "his"—gentleness, she soon became a favorite among her brethren, whom she served with all devotion. From time to time the abbot sent "him" and two monks to a town far away to purchase what was needed in the monastery. They would spend the night in an inn.

The inn owner had a young daughter. One day he discovered to his horror that she was pregnant, and used violence to find out who had brought this shame upon them. Wanting to protect her lover from her father's fury, the girl said, "The young, handsome monk did it to me."

Her father went to the abbot in a rage and complained to him. He in turn questioned Theodora who, thinking that one of "his" fellow monks was responsible, fell on her knees and said, "Forgive me. I am guilty." Knowing that the monk would be expelled from the monastery for this misdeed, Theodora thought, "If he sinned like this as a monk, he will do even worse things when he is dismissed." So she said only, "Forgive me, Father, I have sinned."

"He" was immediately expelled but did not leave the monastery. For years in heat or cold she stood at the gate asking forgiveness from all who came and went. In the end the abbot had pity on her and took her in again, but until the end of her life she was kept at menial work and was not given any consideration. When she died and the corpse had to be washed, according to the monastic rules, it was seen that "he" was a woman. She had taken upon herself another's guilt to keep him in the religious atmosphere of the monastery in the hope that he would not fall even deeper into sin.

The Orthodox church now honors the name of Theodora.

Such deeds are so far beyond what we meet in daily life that you wonder if those who act like this are from our world, or if they receive their inspiration from another realm.

Hannah, a personality of the Old Testament, sang with sadness, "There is none holy like the Lord" (1 Samuel 2:2). This song is tragic. God wishes us all to be holy and perfect like Himself. Jesus is only adored for His love and self-sacrifice, but He would prefer to see His example followed, to be "one among many brethren".

We are all invited to take decisive steps toward this.

~3~

Tso-Po-Tao's Sacrifice

O NCE WHEN PREACHING IN CHINA (TAIWAN), I tried to do so Chinese-style. I told my listeners a story from the Chuen-Chin period of Chinese history (15th B.C.)

Tso-Po-Tao went on a journey with Yang-Chao-Ai, during which they were overtaken by a heavy snowstorm. Unprepared for this, they had neither the clothing nor the food to survive. Tso-Po-Tao offered to undress and give all his clothing and food to Yang-Chao-Ai so that he at least might be saved. Yang refused, but in vain. Tso was already naked and half-frozen. Tso died, and Yang's life was spared.

As is my custom, I had thought much upon my sermon before delivering it. In deep meditation, one has a sense of the reality of the persons who pass through the mind. It was almost as if I had heard with my own ears the words of Tso-Po-Tao: "I give my body for you." I saw him undressing while the snow fell. After removing his jacket and feeling the sharp cold, he surely must have felt a strong temptation to keep at least his shirt for himself. But his face shone more and more. His features became even more determined. He did not stop before he was completely naked, like the first couple in paradise, who had no cause for shame. I marveled at his sacrifice and admired him as Yang-Chao-Ai must have admired him. Certainly his surviving friend would never forget this moment that held the grandeur of eternity.

I read this story decades ago and could never forget it. It represents the pinnacle of what the inner man of the heart longs for.

My audience was moved, too.

Then I paused—what would music be without pauses? Preachers should not go on and on without interruption—I remained a little time in adoration of the God of love, who taught men and women of all ages to ascend to such heights.

After awhile I continued: "As in the case of Tso-Po-Tao who traveled with Yang-Chao-Ai, when righteousness and sin travel together both seem doomed to die. In the storms of life, righteousness does not bear sin, and sin cannot bear righteousness. Therefore Jesus, the embodiment of righteousness, chose to die. He gave more than His food and clothes. He gave His body and blood to the sinner that he might survive. Gratitude for this sacrifice changes hearts. The Chinese character for 'righteousness' is the letter 'I' covered by a lamb. We live by the fact that Jesus, called the Lamb of God because of His meekness, gave Himself for us."

I did not end my sermon with this. I knew some of my listeners had questions: *Could only Tso-Po-Tao before Christ and a limited number of such people after Christ have had such beauty of character, or can we also ascend to such heights? Can we also become masters of love, masters of life, the sort of men and women whom the Bible calls "more than conquerors"—victors over selfishness?*

I have personally known such people. I have known dying men in Communist prisons who gave the medicine that could have saved their lives to another sick prisoner, even to one belonging to a faction utterly opposed to them. I have seen men who were terribly hungry give their last piece of bread to another. I have seen the joy on their faces when they brought the greatest sacrifice. I have heard some of them singing, their faces

RICHARD WURMBRAND

shining like the sun. Can we also become masters of a joy that persists even in the midst of terrible suffering? What is the key to this palace?

Religious people will say it is the grace of God that makes some men stronger and better than others. It does not depend on us.

But the Bible is a Jewish book. The Jewish mind jumps over a whole chain of intermediary events and explains them by their first cause. In Genesis 41:13, we read that a young man by the name of Joseph hanged the baker of an Egyptian king. But in Chapter 40:22, it is written that the one who hanged the baker was the king, not Joseph, who was in prison. This is an insoluble contradiction in the average mind, but not in Jewish thinking. Joseph was the first to inform the baker, with whom he shared prison life, that he would be hanged, so he is considered as the one who hanged him.

In the same way the Bible ascribes to God alone the merit for all the good that is in humanity, but He gives every good thing as a potential. Every child is a potential grownup, but he must do his part in feeding, exercising, and developing his abilities. So we receive goodness, love, self-sacrifice, nobility of character in potential. But these qualities must be learned in the school of hard knocks. How to become a person of great stature must be learned with the same earnestness and persistence with which we learn a trade—overcoming failure, rising after failing again and again, always remembering that the primary source of what is good in us is God.

I feel called to write this book because I knew intimately several such people during my many years of work in the Romanian Underground Church under both Fascism and Communism, as well as in jail. I learned much from them.

I also have first-hand knowledge about others from over 30 years of work with The Voice of the Martyrs, which is in regular contact with the heroes of persecuted churches in all parts of the world.

This book will touch on other subjects as well, but more than anything else it will acquaint you with the Garden of Eden.

Therese of Avila said: "The soul of the righteous is nothing else than a paradise. It is the world that the Heavenly Bridegroom inhabits and in which He rejoices (Proverbs 8:31). How splendid must be a lodging place in which dwells a king so powerful, so wise, so pure, and so rich in all good lives!"

This part of the book will be an ascent to the paradise in which dwell such masters of love and life.

PART 2

THE CONQUERING
POWER OF LOVE

~4~

LOVE CAN MELT SIBERIA'S ICE

GREAT LOVE FOR CHRIST IS ONE OF THE QUICKEST ways to ascend to a mastery of life. One such master is Bishop Victor Belikh, a Ukranian Christian whom I met in Kishinev. He had spent twenty-four years in Communist jails. The first twenty he passed in solitary confinement without ever knowing anything about his family and friends. He was allowed no family visits and no correspondence.

Every evening a straw mattress was put in the cell for him to sleep on for seven hours. In the morning it was taken away. The rest of the time he was not allowed to lie down even on the cold concrete, nor was he allowed to sit or stand still on it. For seventeen hours a day he had to walk around his cell uninterruptedly, as horses do in a circus. He was surveyed by jailers through the peephole in the cell door. If he stopped or broke down, they threw buckets of water on him or beat him and he was forced to continue. After twenty years of such a regime, he was sent for another four years to forced labor in northern Siberia, where the ice never melts.

I asked him, "How could you bear this suffering after the years in solitary confinement and a starvation diet?"

He replied by singing a song he composed: "With the flames of love's fire that Jesus kindled in my heart, I caused the ice of Siberia to melt. Hallelujah!" His face shone. The Bible writes that the face of Stephen, first martyr of Christianity, shone when he was sentenced to death.

I did not feel worthy to stand before such a man. What an honor Jesus gave me to be called a "brother in faith" by such a man, to have become a member of a family that breeds such exemplary humans! But more than that, the possibility is given to each of us to become such conquerors of life. This is not only the grace of God but also assiduous work on your own character. It is as if at birth we are given a block of marble, a hammer, a chisel, and are told, "You can hew out of this the image of an emperor." Jesus does not wish to be the only most holy Person, but the first among many brothers and sisters of the same kind. We are all called to be holy.

Men put into Belikh's situation are rare, but many men in deportation, in labor camps, in places devastated by war and revolution, even many poor in rich countries, have no shelter from the cold. But there is another kind of cold. It is often icy cold in well-to-do homes. Love has grown cold. There is no longer a smile or pleasant gesture for those who were once loved. Spouses, parents, children, friends have become alienated from each other.

In Jesus' time there was no electricity. The smallest light had to be kept burning. There were not even matches to kindle a fire. One had to be very thrifty. Jesus says about himself that "He will not quench a smoking flax." When I was in jail, we blew again and again on what seemed no more than the remembrance of a fire that had gone out, and we succeeded in bringing it to life again. If everyone around you is icy, don't despair. Ice can be made to melt if the fire of Jesus' love burns in your heart.

~5~

Loving While Suffering

*S*UFFERING TORMENTS SOME SOULS, AND DRIVES some to despair and even suicide. Others are grateful for it. I have seen faithful Christian prisoners dancing for joy. They have recognized God as almighty and in patience they show love toward the evil men who torture them. They know this love of God is irresistible. It will conquer.

Even the best of Christians are troubled by the question, "Why does an almighty God send, or at least allow, suffering?" When you are nagged by thoughts like this, say to yourself, "I am still in elementary school. When I graduate from the university of Christian life, I will understand His ways better and doubts will cease."

We do not have the right notion of might, which to us means the power to crush, to subdue, to suppress, to punish. There exists another might—it is the might to love, to be patient and quiet, to suffer innocently, and to be good to the wrongdoer. When we think about energy, we think of it as kinetic, a quality that makes all things move. But there exists the huge reservoir of potential energy, of energy at rest. There exists the power of quietness, of serenity.

A Communist officer told a Christian while beating him, "I am almighty, as you suppose your God to be. I can kill you."

The Christian answered, "The power is all on my side. I can love you while you torture me to death."

Such is God's almightiness—it is reflected in the deep tranquility of the souls of saints. They do not ask the troublesome question, "Why all the sorrow?"—they have learned to love the cross and to be rejected without comfort. Once you take this attitude, the perplexity ceases. What child is troubled when he receives a much desired gift?

The peak of holiness is never to ask anything for yourself, never to refuse a cross with which God honors you, and to accept life meekly as it comes, without questions. We are not ready to understand the answers yet. Some day we will know as also we are known by God (2 Corinthians 13:12).

Saints are not people who have much light from God. They are nothings through whom shines God's power to endure, to hope, and to love even the worst of people. Who knows if the murderer of today will not be a future apostle, if today's loose woman will not be a Magdalene? And cannot God compensate in eternity the wrong suffered here for a little while?

We bless the Father, the Son, and the Holy Ghost. We say to the Lord, "Blessed is the womb that bore thee" (Luke11:27) and advance on the path of faith, without tormenting ourselves with many "Whys" about suffering, which we welcome because in them we can glorify Christ joyfully.

How impressive is the prayer of a woman in the camp of Vorkuta in Siberia:

> "O God, accept all my sufferings, my tiredness, my humiliations, my tears, my nostalgia, my being hungry, my suffering of cold, all the bitterness accumulated in my soul. . . . Dear Lord, have pity also on those who persecute and torture us day and night. Grant them, too, the divine grace of knowing the sweetness and happiness of your love."

-6-

"Baptize Me or I'll Shoot!"

Those who are badly hurt in the free world usually try to escape from their tormentors. Not so with Annmarie, a young Slovak Christian, While she was being tortured, her main desire was to prevent her torturer from going to perdition. She shared with him again and again the beauty of Christ and His kingdom. His reply was more punches and more whipping, to which she responded by using every pause in the beating to bring him to God.

The holy word worked in the criminal. Once when she was brought before him, he asked her in mockery, "Tell me more about your God." Torturers often got tired of beating and would take coffee breaks. During these pauses, they were ready, while smoking, to listen, to be entertained. Annmarie complied with his request, adding, "In vain you beat me. You will never succeed in beating out of me my love for God nor my ardent love for you."

He mocked her: "Usually girls wait for boys to declare their love first. What is this stupid declaration of love on your part? We are not in the love business here. You should be telling me the secrets of the Underground Church. If you don't, I will beat out of you all your loves, for God, for me, or for other young men."

She replied, "While you beat me, I looked at your hands. They are beautiful. I imagine how your wife enjoys it when you use them to caress her. When one caresses, two persons have pleasure, the caressed and the one caressing. But what is the good of beating? It is terrible for those of us who are victims. But it must be terrible for you too to have your ears deafened with cries of suffering. And this day by day, every day. It must be maddening. So why don't you turn from beating to caressing?

"I will tell you one thing more, something no girl normally tells a young man. But here we are in extraordinary circumstances. You have very attractive lips. How happy your wife must be when you kiss her; what rapture this must be for both of you. May I ask you a simple question? Isn't kissing better than swearing, shouting foul words, or being angry? Both you and the person you address are soiled by such language. Then why not kissing instead of swearing? God created our lips for this."

"Where do you get all these foolish thoughts?" he asked.

She replied, "I have a boyfriend, the sweetest of all. Not that He loves me. He is love, the most exquisite love, love of a kind that does not seek pleasure so much as to fill the beloved with joy. Since knowing this boyfriend, I too can only love. Whether I am caressed or hurt, I can only love. You love hatred now. I call upon you to love Love."

He gave her a powerful blow, and she fell to the concrete, hitting her temple and passing out. When she came to, she saw him sitting quietly as if in meditation. He told her, "I have been thinking about your boyfriend. What He says makes sense. Caressing is better than beating and kissing is better than swearing. I'm surprised that this simple truth has not been obvious to me before. Who is this boyfriend of yours?"

Annmarie told him the Name above every name.

He asked simply, "How can I make Him be my friend too?"

She replied, "You must repent and be baptized."

"Then baptize me immediately," he demanded.

She replied, "I can't do that!" She did not know that in special circumstances everyone can baptize, even a child.

He pointed a revolver at her: "Baptize me now or I'll shoot you!"

The words seem strange, but they fulfill precisely the words of Jesus, "The kingdom of heaven suffers violence, and the violent take it by force" (Matthew 10:12). This man wanted the kingdom forcefully and was ready to shoot his way into it.

He dragged her to a pool and dumped her into the water, following after. Annmarie baptized him. After a time, the converted torturer, risking his own liberty, gave her the certificate of release from jail of another woman prisoner who had died the day she was to be set free.

PART 3

ASCENDING

7

The Simplest Way to Obtain God's Love

THERE ARE HUNDREDS OF WAYS TO OBTAIN GOD'S love, but only one is certain," said a preacher.

"What's that?" asked a colleague.

"Allen" retorted the first, "I *thought* you wouldn't know."

The least-known way to obtain God's love is the simplest one: to keep His commandments. Jesus said, "He that has my commandments, and keeps them, he it is that loves me; and he that loves me shall be loved of my Father, and I will love Him" (John 14:21). He also said, "If you will enter into life, keep the commandments" (Matthew 19:17). Every morning, sing a hymn, read a Bible portion, pray, have a quiet time for listening to what God has to say to you that day, and then set about to fulfill His commands. All His commandments can be resolved into one: to be like Jesus and the best of men, even though this might involve suffering and possibly death.

In the battle of Waterloo, Napoleon was defeated by the British general Wellington. Lord Hill, showing the latter the corpse of his aide-de-camp Gordon, asked: "What is your instruction, my lord, if *you* are killed?"

The answer was brief: "Do the same as I would."

Jesus died for the glory of the Father and commands all His disciples to die to sin (Romans 6:2), and to lose, if necessary, their natural life in obedience to the commandments. The Bible teaches, "This is the law: when a man dies . . ." (Numbers 19:14).

A religion is truly religion if you are ready to die for it. What is not worthy of the sacrifice of life is not religion. Your desire to lead a consistent Christian life might lead to renunciation and heavy losses. Jesus was ready to die on a cross at the age of thirty-three, and we are meant to be like Him in dedication to God and love toward our fellow men. Whoever keeps this commandment is His beloved.

The Church urges us to a heroic Christian life. One of the names of Jesus is "Heroic God" (Isaiah 9:6, in Hebrew).

$-8-$

WE CAN ASCEND FROM THE WORST DEPTHS

OME OF US LIVE VERY FAR FROM SUCH HEIGHTS OF love. Some of us wallow in great sin. But some very depraved people have moments of grandeur. There is just a little seed of good in them, but eventually it could grow.

The Talmud, the holy book of the Jews, contains the following story:

Once during a drought, Rabbi Abahu heard a voice: "If Pentikaka [which means in Greek, *five evils*] prayed, it would rain."

Abahu asked Pentikaka about his occupation. He replied, "I provide men with prostitutes, I clean the theater, I take the clothes of prostitutes to the laundry, I dance and play the cymbals before them."

The rabbi asked, "Did you ever do good?"

He replied, "While I cleaned the theater, I saw a woman weeping. She told me, 'My husband is in prison. I will prostitute myself and rescue him.' Then I sold all I had, even the blanket, and gave the money to the woman. I told her, 'Take this, ransom him, and don't sin.'"

Hearing this, Rabbi Abahu exclaimed, "His prayer is worthy to be accepted."

Such hidden possibilities exist even in bad men.

In Romania, Berila was given a life sentence for murdering a couple and their four children—the youngest only a baby—to steal a small sum of money for drink. He had even killed their cat. A baker by profession, he worked in the prison bakery where bread, biscuits, and cakes were made for the prison staff. Berila risked heavy beatings by bringing to hungry prisoners some of the bakery products reserved only for officers and wardens.

But whence this gem in a dirty place? Could I also be such a jewel? Am I, too, called to ascend?

This is not a book that simply tells a good person how to become better. Those who have wings can fly from peak to peak, each higher than the last. Those who do not can ascend from a deep pit on a ladder, slowly, rung by rung. The Bible uses both these images.

Many former criminals have become exemplary saints.

~9~

PSYCHOTHERAPIST'S SOUL HEALED

KASPAROVITCH, ONE OF THE MOST FAMOUS Soviet psychotherapists, had been educated in atheism like everyone else in Russia. But now that religion is free in that benighted country, he received for the first time a Gospel tract. In it he found two of Jesus' sayings, through which, he says, God revealed himself to him. The first was, "Not as I will, but as you will" (Matthew 26:39). In this he found the key to a healthy mental life and to healthy relations with others.

Two wills operate in a person's life: that of his own consciousness and that of his Creator. The former appeared yesterday and will disappear tomorrow. It knows as much as a toddler knows. It is determined by the passions, impulses, interests, and pleasures of the self, which must come to realize its own pettiness and unreliability. Therefore it has to say, "Not my will" but "The will of my all-knowing Creator, who loves me and has a host of angels to fulfill His plans for my life."

The experience is like that of a patient who surrenders his consciousness to an anesthetist and surgeon to do with his body what they know to be best. Not the will of the sick, but that of the surgeon. Not my will, but that of God.

Jesus' words, "Not as I will, but as you will," apply not only to God but also to relations between people. Our guide in life should be, "Not my will, but as my spouse, my child, my parents, my boss, my employee, the man with whom I am in conflict wills—providing it does not harm them."

Accept these words of Jesus, and you too will be healthy.

Kasparovitch was also struck by Jesus' expressed purpose in His earthly life: "I came not to destroy, but to fulfill," "I came not to judge, but to save," and "I came to seek and to save that which was lost."

Jesus knew why He came into the world. There is a purpose also in our appearing in the world. We must fulfill the law of love. If we live according to this law, we will be happy and will make others happy. Through Christ's love in us, we will ascend higher into the paradise of God while still on this earth.

~10~

PATIENCE WITH THOSE WHO WAVER

*S*INCE NOT ALL WHO WERE PERSECUTED FOR THEIR faith were strong or bore their cross with dignity and resisted temptation—like us in the free world?—how should we relate to them?

Over 700 years before the coming of Jesus, Isaiah prophesied the appearance of a servant of God in whose name the Gentiles would trust: "A bruised reed shall he not break, and smoking flax shall he not quench, till he send forth judgment unto victory" (Matthew 12:20).

Often quoted to show the merciful nature of the Lord, these words should speak to us in a more profound way than just make us beg for His pity. In our age of readily available fire, from matches to blow-torches, it is hard to imagine how important it was in the primitive society of Isaiah's time for someone not to quench smoking flax. But anyone who has tried to light a campfire when the wood was drenched by rain, or depended on a last match, realizes that in order to start a fire it is not enough to leave smoking twigs or leaves alone, even briefly. One has to blow repeatedly and inhale smoke for a long period, starting and restarting the fire until blood rushes to the head and one feels dizzy. Even in a dry house, the effort needed to start a fire in the fireplace or a primitive stove is considerable, especially if a person is trembling with the cold. Such is the price for keeping smoking flax from being quenched. For in those times, fire was left overnight to smoulder in the ashes so that it could be more easily rekindled the next morning.

The first disciples spoke of this from their own familiar experience. Jesus must have kept many a fire from being quenched, most of them spiritually, but some even physically. Even after His resurrection, He waited for them on the shores of Lake Tiberias with a fire on which fish were being broiled (John 21:9). This must have been a pleasant surprise for the disciples after a whole night of unsuccessful fishing. All true followers of Jesus also work hard, giving their breath to fan into flame the tiny sparks in the ashes of another's life.

Communists who burned genitals with red-hot iron pokers were able to break even a cardinal. When a Catholic receives a cardinal's beret, the Pope tells him that this is to be a sign that he will defend the faith *usque ad sanguem,* to the blood. But a cardinal confessed at his trial to having been a spy and a black marketeer.

The effects of brainwashing last many years. Another cardinal, in Rome after eighteen years in Soviet jails, declared: "The Catholic is nowhere in opposition to authority. This certainly applies to the Soviet regime." It was not the cardinal who said this, but the Communist brainwasher who had programmed him to do so.

In Russia, Alexander Ogorodnikov organized a Christian seminar. For this he received a mild sentence: one year. But when he had finished this term, he was tried once more for having preached about Christ in prison. The public, gathered in the courtyard of the tribunal, was not allowed to enter. Ogorodnikov opened the window near the dock and shouted the story of Christ to the crowd. For this he was given another six years, which he served. But then three more years were added on.

He then wrote a depressing letter to his mother. Heroes too have their memories of despair when it seems to them that everything is lost. Jesus himself cried out on the Cross, "My God, my God, why have you forsaken me?" Ogorodnikov said he was kept in punishment cells at 30-degrees Fahrenheit. He hoped for death, as the end of pain. He even cut his veins, but was discovered. We should not judge him. The spirit is strong but the flesh is weak. It was after a long hunger strike that he yielded to despair—he had demanded a Bible but was refused.

What really brought him to desperation, however, was the silence around him. Like all of us, he was hungry for love. Attempts at suicide and harsh words are often simply the expression of one desire: "Show me love and recognition."

In the letter to his mother he wrote:

> Men are so terribly tortured that they wish for death, and no one cares. Soldiers hopelessly wounded are shot to free them from pain, whereas I have to endure it lifelong. Suicide is a terrible, unpardonable sin. I have committed it. If the persecutors killed me, they would free me from suffering. Only publicity can save me, and this is possible only through you.
>
> Why don't you write me at least to tell me if my son Dima goes to church, takes Communion, wears a cross? He should not enter the Communist children's organization, because he is a Christian. If you don't write me, I will give myself entirely into the hands of the torturers without protesting. Your silence is a stab in my back.
>
> It is difficult to realize that you are not needed by anyone, that you are destined to forgo a life full of energy without receiving sympathy, that you must hunger, suffer cold, be deprived of books. That even life, God's holy gift, must consist of blank pain.
>
> May God protect you.

The apostle Paul knew that the best of men pass through such times of despondency, so he wrote: "Strengthen the hands which hang down, and the feeble knees" (Hebrews 12:12).

Our mission published Ogorodnikov's letter in many countries, along with his address. We also printed a letter from another prisoner who, when freed, returned to a hungry family with nothing to give him. Neighbors helped with a few potatoes. These, cooked without any fat, were his first meal after years of starvation. As a result, some of our readers wrote to these sufferers. Their letters and the information that their families would be cared for lifted the spirits of these despairing souls and gave them hope.

The same Ogorodnikov who wrote a despondent letter later communicated the following:

I bow my head and bend my knees with profound gratitude for your prayers and compassionate activity in defense of the persecuted Russian Christians. In the concentration camps, buried in the gravelike darkness of solitary cells, in the silence that changes even time into torture, when silent yearning erodes the heart, hungry, when it seems that the world has forgotten you—I felt physically how your prayers warmed me in the cold of my cell, tying us together in our common faith. Your hand passed through the high wall and barbed wire. The power of your love changed my despair to undefeatable hope. The all-seeing God heard your prayers and opened the prison gates. We see now how your love, faith, and works change history.

–11–

LET US GO HIGHER UP

AT THIS TIME IT IS 1993, AND I AM NOW 83 years old. In the Bible there is a man called Barzillai who is described as "very old," though he was only 80. My life has also been full of suffering, and even now I have many burdens to bear. So it is natural for me to ask myself if I will be able to write this new book.

When General Morescat told Napoleon that the crossing of the Alps would be very difficult, the Emperor asked, "But is it possible?"

The general replied, "If you make an extraordinary effort."

"Then let us go," said Napoleon.

Napoleon's army had to cross to the other side of the Alps. I, too, have to cross a barrier, and I would like us to make the crossing together.

In several places, the gospel tells about Jesus' commandment to His disciples "to depart or go before Him to the other side" (of the sea of Galilee). At other times he accompanies them.

The Bible has a mystical as well as a historical meaning. Though we live on earth, we sometimes have to move to another realm. This was true of the apostle Paul and his companions when they were in jail. For certain periods they were raptured to heavenly places. There were hours of relaxation when they were surrounded not by jailers and torturers, but by angels. Then they had to "cross the sea" again and return to the material world with its locked doors, iron bars, whips, and crosses. After a time there would be another crossing back to the world of the spirit.

Under both Fascism and Communism I endured suffering and strife, and I am sure that those of you who lived in the free world have had your crosses, too. But the purpose of this book is to elevate ourselves—author and reader alike—to the higher realm in which all that is petty in human life is conquered, to a place from which we can better view our lives, our churches, and our countries.

This journey will not be easy, but with God's help we may succeed.

PART 4

JOURNEYS INTO GLORY

12

LIKE THE DAY OF ANNUNCIATION

WHEN I WAS IN PRISON, A YOUNG CELLMATE Jon Lugajanu was taken to court. When he returned, his face shone. The other prisoners asked what happened.

He answered, "It was like the day of Mary's annunciation. What a beautiful day! A pure virgin sits alone in meditation. At once a radiant angel stands before her. He tells her that she, a creature, will have the Creator as a baby in her arms; that she, a creature, will wash her Creator; that she will wash the One who afterwards will wash millions of men from their sins. She, a creature, will teach her Creator to walk. She will teach the eternal Word of God to speak. He will be the sun and joy of her house. There will be a few difficult moments. She will have to stand weeping at the foot of a Cross where God's Son and her Son will die for our salvation, but this will pass. He will be resurrected and will go to heaven and, surely, He will call His mother to be with Him. And it will be joy again, without end."

The prisoners thanked him for the nice little sermon, but they insisted, "We asked you something else. How was it in court?"

He repeated, "I told you already. It was like the day of Mary's annunciation. It was announced that I am sentenced to death. Is it not beautiful? Gates of pearl, streets of gold, angels playing harps, the communion of saints, and above all, rest on Jesus' bosom."

This is how suffering and death are received by Christians in Communist countries. How much we can learn from them!

-13-

Lost Lives Can No Longer Be Lost

*I*N BULGARIA, IN THE PRISON OF BELEN, THERE WAS a pit with hungry dogs. Naked prisoners were thrown into it if they broke some prison rule. In some cases God performed miracles. Brother Trofim Dimitrov was thrown to the dogs. While being led to the place, he prayed for his enemies, who threw him into the pit. Immediately a great howling was heard. When the officers looked into the pit, they saw Brother Dimitrov kneeling in prayer and the dogs in panic, barking and trying to jump the walls in order to save themselves from the strange power emanating from him. It remains God's mystery why He performs such miracles for some, whereas others have to drink the bitter cup until the end.

In Cuba, there were some 30,000 political prisoners, which includes those sentenced for their faith. In a document smuggled out of Cuban prisons, we were told that our brethren, among others, were forced into an ice-cold shower followed by a hot one. After being thus treated, they had sulphur thrown on them to make their skin burn. Bodies of prisoners were crushed with bulldozers.

In Hungary, the abbot Roman Braga, my former fellow-prisoner, wrote about a Christian to whom the Communists, with revolvers in their hands, offered the alternatives of raping his daughter or shooting him. He chose the latter.

I was sometimes accused of dramatizing the situation in Eastern countries, but who in the world can dramatize what is already an unequaled drama?

A Soviet newspaper described certain Christians as "men who have lost the human image" and claimed that:

> *They destroy their brethren and sisters from their denomination and other witnesses who are dangerous to them. So at the liquidation of secret "death chambers" of the* Innokentists [the Innocents—a specific Russian Christian group] *approximately twenty corpses of men, women, and children between the ages of 14 and 50 were discovered. Many of them had been buried alive. In such sects, men are exhausted through fasting, the forbidding of meat and other nutritious produces, and through the ascetic form of life. The heavy, oppressive, conditions in the sectarian communities often lead to crimes or psychic illness* (Sovietskaia Moldavia, *January 16, 1973).*

These Christians had allegedly been killed by their own brethren. Christians in the Soviet Union were sometimes charged with ritual murder—that is, with the accusation that in order to receive forgiveness of sins from God they kill a member of the Church. This was the first time, however, that we found Christians charged not with murdering one individual, but with ritual mass murder.

Everywhere in the world it is known that Jesus taught Christians to love and to save lives. Only in the Communist camp is the lie spread that at their religious services they kill. In the fifties, in Red China, Catholic nuns were accused of having killed children in hospitals. Nowhere else in the world are nuns charged with such activity. Such monstrous accusations brought against Christians were simply ridiculous.

Soviet Christians have no lives of their own to lose. From the hell of Soviet prisons, a believer smuggled out the following letter, which shows a heart full of peace and adoration that doesn't even seem to be aware of the horrors in the environment.

"Marvellous are thy works" (Psalm 139:14). I greet and congratulate you with these words, dear mother and dear daughter, on your birthday. This was the text of the first cable in the world, in 1845—a verse from the Bible. The inventor of the telegraph was Samuel Morse. As to his father George Morse, it is significant that he was a renowned evangelist. This Bible text was written 3,000 years ago and entered so deeply into the hearts of many generations of men with a living faith in God that it was transcribed faultlessly by hand during 2,500 years. In 1455, it was first printed. The first printed book was the Bible.

The works of God are really marvelous in all things, in nature and technique, in the lives of all men, in the destiny of people and of mankind, and especially of His church. It is a great joy to contemplate the work of His hand and of His creative mind in all that surrounds us. The Bible is also the first book from which men read when circling around the moon . . .

I see from your letters that you are very troubled because of me. My beloved, this should not be. Keep your health, and don't let your heart be troubled. May it be in perfect peace, because everything happens according to His will.

Soviet Christians see God's will and good intentions even while bearing Communist atrocities, whereas unbelievers or those who believe superficially say to Jesus, "Depart from us— you made us lose a herd of swine" (see Mark 5:14-17).

This book is written with the purpose of offering readers, all of whom encounter hardships in life, though not like the foregoing, the perfect calm of sufferers for Christ. Such calm is a gift of God, but it needs to be cultivated.

~14~

BAPTIST CONFESSORS

HE BULLETIN OF THE COUNCIL OF RELATIVES OF Christian Prisoners in the Soviet Union published excerpts of the protocol of a trial.

Brother George Jeltonoshko and Sister Nadeja Troshtshenko were brought before court in Nikolaiev, accused of having spread Bibles, Gospels and spiritual literature.

Jeltonoshko told the court: "I refuse to have a lawyer. I feel I am right. Righteousness needs no defense." (Why do we all attempt to defend ourselves so much when accused?)

The judge asked him, "Do you plead guilty?"

He answered: "No! To spread Christian literature is the duty of a Christian."

The Communist judge asked him to follow the example of the traitors from the official church who respect the Soviet law and do not propagate the gospel.

Jeltonoshko answered that he could not do like them because Christ had said, "Go into the whole world and preach."

The Communist judge took the defense of the official churches, which compromised with Communism, while the Underground churches did not, and asked again, "Why don't you remain in the official churches? They also consist of believers."

He answered, "The devils also believe and tremble."

The judge was inquisitive, "Where do you meet for prayers?"

His answer was, "True worshipers worship everywhere."

At this trial Sister Zinaida Kozakova was mentioned. She had distributed among the Red Army, leaflets entitled, *Spiritual Passport*. This is what they contained:

> *Name:* Christian.
>
> *Father's name:* God.
>
> *Last name:* Blessed.
>
> *Date of Birth:* Now is the accepted time; behold, now is the time of salvation.
>
> *Country of origin:* The holy land.
>
> *Town:* Jerusalem.
>
> *Nationality:* New creation.
>
> *Profession:* Co-worker with God.
>
> *Military duty:* Good soldier of Christ.
>
> *Passport issued by whom:* By faith.
>
> *On the basis of what documents was the passport issued:* Love believes everything.
>
> *To what social category do you belong, rich, poor, or middle class:* In everything we are enriched by Christ.
>
> *Property:* I possess all things present and future.
>
> *Family:* A great multitude.
>
> *Education:* We know all things (1 John 2:20).
>
> *Profession:* Prayer and the service of the Word.

What was the price of faithfully teaching the Scriptures? Jeltonoshko was sentenced to three years of prison, Troshtshenko to eighteen months. But it is not the length of the prison term that counts, but the prison regime. In a Soviet jail, no prisoner is allowed to share his beliefs with anyone else. The punishments for doing so are so vicious that in one concentration camp fifteen prisoners sewed their lips together in protest against the terror.

-15-

MARTYRS OF THE ORTHODOX CHURCH

A BOOK, *GIVE THEM PEACE WITH THE SAINTS*, secretly compiled by the True Orthodox Church of the Soviet Union, provides the following accounts.

The first Orthodox priest ever killed by the Communists was John Kotchurov. In Essentuke, the priest John Riabuhin, together with many others, had his limbs hacked off and was buried while still breathing. The priest John Krasnov was burned alive in a ship's cauldron. The priest Alexander Podolskii was beaten to death. Those who tried to bury him were shot. The deacon Tikhon sang his own burial service, while his son, aged ten, dug his grave, being compelled by the Reds to do so.

The priest Grigorii Dmitrevskii first had his nose and ears cut off, then his head (exactly what the Communist guerrillas did in Rhodesia). The priest Grigorii Nikolski was shot with a bullet through his mouth after saying the liturgy. The murderers told him, "Now we will give you holy Communion."

The secret police went to search the house of Antonii, the Orthodox bishop of Arkhangelsk. Finding the vessel for holy communion, they threw it to the floor and stomped on it. The bishop threw himself over it, trying to defend it with his body. In the scuffle he lost consciousness. When he awoke he was in jail.

They asked his opinion about the future of the Russian church and wanted to know if he desired the overthrow of the Soviets. He answered that the Church would be glorified through the suffering of its martyrs, as in the first centuries, and that he prayed daily that the Soviet government would not shed blood and would be forgiven of its sins.

First he was threatened with death, then was promised freedom if he would become an informer for the police. The bishop was not frightened and could not be bought. Such is the character of all those who see afar, who see the heavenly city where believers will spend eternity.

He was put in a small cell together with five others. They endured bitter cold, received only two glasses of water a day and nothing else. They could not wash or change their clothes, and lived in their stench. They lost their teeth. The bishop became so weak that he could not cleanse his beard from the invading bugs and lice. When he felt death near, he chanted his own funeral service. He died with prayers on his lips.

Fyodor Dostoyevsky (1821-1881), the greatest Russian writer, wrote:

> *I believe there is nothing lovelier, deeper, more sympa-*
> *thetic and more perfect than Jesus. I say to myself with*
> *jealous love that not only is there no one else like Him,*
> *but there could be no one. I would say even more. If*
> *anyone could prove to me that Christ is outside the*
> *truth, and if the truth did really exclude Christ, I*
> *should prefer to stay with Christ and not with truth.*
> *There is in the world only one figure of absolute*
> *beauty: Christ.*

So the complete works of Dostoyevsky had to be forbidden in Russia. It is like forbidding Shakespeare in English-speaking countries. Eugen Vaghin, who published Dostoyevsky, got thirteen years of prison, which meant thirteen years of torture. A document later proved that one of the punishments inflicted in jail was exposure of naked prisoners to mosquitoes. The prisoners had their hands handcuffed behind them so that they were unable to defend themselves from the mosquitoes' bites.

Vaghin survived fourteen years of such imprisonment. When he was freed, he was still enamored of Jesus, just as he had been when he gave up everything for Him.

~16~

HEROES IN THE
WORST OF HORRORS

*N*O ONE WILL EVER BE ABLE TO DESCRIBE ALL the horrors of Communism. Edward Buca, a former inmate of Soviet concentration camps, describes in his book, *Vorkuta*, a particular horror. A Communist police officer tied a woman down, gagged her, and then took a large candle and pushed it into her private parts and lit it. He told the woman, "You have a little time to think things over. Soon the flame will reach your body. When you're ready to sign the confession, give me the signal by blinking three times." As the flame burned down to her body, he watched calmly. Once he took out the candle, lit a cigarette with it, and put it back.

Prisoners who had tried to escape were beaten savagely, then tied behind galloping reindeer and dragged to death. A prisoner was compelled to play the harmonica near the corpses, which had been exposed to public view.

More gruesome horrors can scarcely be imagined.

But this is only one side of the story. I would never have told it, were there not a transcendent side that more than compensates for the ugliness.

In the third volume of his book, *Gulag Archipelago,* Solzhenitsyn tells the story of an evangelist whose name "seems to have been Alexander Sisoiev." He never published volumes of sermons, was never on television, had no mass rallies. Just as the creed says nothing about the sermons of Jesus but only that He suffered under Pontius Pilate, was crucified and buried, so history says about Sisoiev only that he was an evangelist and that he was shot in the Kengir concentration camp, after spending many years in prison in quiet communion with his Lord. At that time, shooting of the innocent was an everyday occurrence. But this man who "seems to have been Alexander Sisoiev" had been a man apart. Those who looked at him "took knowledge that he had been with Jesus," though he was "unlearned and ignorant" like Peter and John (Acts 4:13).

The camp inmates were resigned to the beating and shooting of other prisoners, but when this saint—whose name is not even known for sure—was shot, the whole camp of 2,500 prisoners—among whom were murderers, burglars, thieves, and 500 political prisoners—rebelled. They refused to work and attacked the guards. Their supreme request was that the person responsible for the shooting be punished.

In the end, the Communists quenched the revolt after killing about 700 political prisoners and criminals, who died showing their love and solidarity for a man about whom we know nothing except that he knew how to maintain his privacy, how to commune in quietness with God, and had an inner prayer closet even in a common prison cell.

Perhaps instead of having conferences about modern evangelization methods it is more important for us to be like the one who "seems to have been Alexander Sisoiev."

I picked this case at random from countless such stories we have heard. I could as well have spoken about Zdorovets, who was terribly beaten in a Soviet prison; or Dubizki, to whom poison was administered in jail; or Peter Siemens, whom the Communist poisoners call "a poisoner of souls" in their newspaper because he brought people to Christ. For this he was sentenced to three years in prison.

These Christians are great not for what they wrote or spoke, for we do not know their words. But we do know that they spent much time alone with the Lord, and as a result they shine now like stars in the firmament of the gospel and in the memory of their fellow prisoners.

Mark's Gospel says, "Without a parable Jesus spoke not unto them" (Mark 4:34). Every parable of Jesus has a streak of sadness in it. We know Jesus wept, whereas we have no report that He ever laughed or smiled. He must feel uneasy around politicians and evangelists who have a professional smile on their lips. In one parable He says a sower must count on the sad fact that three-quarters of his seed will be lost, and then says that a grain of mustard seed grows out of all proportion and becomes a tree (Mark 4). Such fantastic growth of plants has taken place only after the explosion of atomic bombs in Japan. Tragedy also makes the mustard seed of the Kingdom of Heaven grow exceptionally high. The Church grows exceedingly when it is watered by the blood of martyrs.

All Christians must be prepared to face adversity and personal trauma. God can protect us and give us happy days, but no believer is exempt from tribulations. Let us expect them with serenity.

-17-

TRANSPARENT ANGELS

*I*N 1973, VANYA MOISEEV, A YOUNG ROMANIAN, died a martyr's death in the former USSR. His life can serve as a model for us.

Vanya was a soldier in the Soviet army who had the same faith we all have, but with a difference: his faith was contagious. If one has the flu, the chances are that someone else will catch it. So it is with faith.

Vanya spoke about his faith to his comrades and officers. Then he sang about the glory of Christ in his barracks, though this was strictly prohibited. To those who threatened him he replied, "A lark threatened with death for singing would still continue to sing. She cannot renounce her nature. Neither can we Christians." His singing brought fellow soldiers to Christ. For punishment he was forced to stand all night long outside the barracks in the depth of winter, clothed only in a summer uniform. He was flogged and finally stabbed in the heart, just like Jesus, whose heart was pierced by a sword—thus he too had an imprint of Jesus' wound.

He took all the suffering valiantly, saying that an angel had shown him heavenly Jerusalem. An uncultured man, he described angels as no theologian would have done. He said,

"Angels are transparent. If an angel stands before you with a man behind him, the presence of the angel does not keep you from seeing the man. On the contrary: looking at a man through an angel makes him more beautiful. I see my torturers through an angel. In that way, even they become lovable."

People have arbitrarily declared that angels are invisible. Yet Jesus said to Nathaniel, "You shall see angels of God" (John 1:51). If he could see them, why can't we? But you have to understand that they are transparent. Every time you saw the good side of a person you once rejected as totally despicable, an angel was standing between and he altered your perception.

Liuba Ganevskaya was arrested for her faith by Russian Communists. She was kept in a solitary cell, starved, and beaten. One night she said to herself, "Enough is enough. I will not take the blows meekly any more. Tonight, if they begin again, I will tell the police officer to his face that he is a criminal." But that night when he insulted her with foul words and was ready to jump at her, somehow she saw him differently. She observed for the first time that he was as tired of beating her as she was of being beaten. She was worn out from lack of sleep, and so was he. He was as desperate over not obtaining from her the denunciation of others that he expected as she was about suffering for refusing to comply.

A voice told her, "He is so much like you. You are both caught in the same drama of life. Stalin, the chief Communist dictator, killed thousands of God's children, but he also killed 10,000 officers of his own secret police. Three successive heads of police, Yagoda, Yezhov, and Beria, were shot by their comrades, just like the Christians they had persecuted. You and your torturers pass through the same vale of tears."

Liuba looked up at the one who had already lifted the whip to beat her and smiled. Stunned, he asked her, "Why do you smile?"

She replied, "I don't see you as a mirror would reflect you right now. I see you as you surely once were, a beautiful, innocent child. We are the same age. We could have been playmates. Jesus likened those who would later whip and crucify Him to children (Matthew 12:17). I see you, too, as I hope you will be. There was once a persecutor worse than you, Saul of Tarsus, and he became an apostle and a saint."

Liuba had seen a transparent angel.

She asked the now pacified torturer what burden so weighed on him that it drove him to the madness of beating a person who had done him no harm. Because of her loving concern, he became a changed man. She had walked in a manner worthy of God.

We, too, should look like that at spouses, children, parents, brothers, sisters, men and women of other religions, party, class, or race with whom we are in conflict. If we find ourselves beginning to understand, love, and forgive them, then we may know that we have perhaps seen a transparent angel.

-18-

RENOWNED BEGGAR IN CHURCH HISTORY

J. TAULER, THE RENOWNED PRIEST AND THEOLOGIAN whom the reformer Martin Luther called his teacher, felt that he did not have the real thing—intimacy with Christ—and prayed for years for an encounter with somebody who did. There was nobody among his colleagues.

One day, he heard a voice: "Go to that church and you will find the one whom you seek."

He went. At the porch was a beggar in rags. Tauler said, "Good day."

"I don't remember ever having had a bad day," the beggar responded.

"Well, may you have a happy life."

The beggar said, "I was never unhappy. All my days were good. I praised God when I was hungry, when it rained and snowed, and when I was homeless. When I am despised or encounter any other evil, I don't cease to give thanks to God. I am always happy, because I will, without any reservation, all that God wills for me. I receive with joy from God whatever He gives me, be it sweet or bitter. This makes me happy."

Wow!

Tauler asked him, "What would you do if you were damned for eternity?"

"I have two arms: humility and love. With these I would embrace Him so mightily that if I had to enter hell, He would have to enter with me. It would be sweeter for me to be with Him in hell than without Him in heaven."

"When did you find God?"

"When I forsook attachment to any creature."

"But who are you?"

"I am a king."

"Where is your kingdom?"

"It is right in my heart. Christ gave it to me when He shed His blood for me."

The churches that have passed through persecution have such saints. The Lutheran pastor Traugott Hahn, who was killed by the Communists in Latvia in 1919, was one. He once wrote:

> *Higher Christianity starts only where martyrdom and sacrifice start. Without sacrifice, there is no salvation. It is foolishness to wish happiness on earth. Life is self-denial. To put everything at stake for God and His Church, to follow Him to the very end, is more than happiness. It is bliss.*

–19–

MARTYRS AT
DIFFERENT LEVELS

*I*VAN HOREV DIED FOR CHRIST IN JAIL. HIS SON Nikolai also went to jail for twenty years.

It is a rule that when an officer enters a cell everyone has to stand to attention. Once, Nikolai Horev was slow to show such respect. For this he was punished with a hundred days in solitary, in which food was given only every second day. After this, a new torture called, "Afrikanka," was applied to him. He was put barefoot in a box with room only to stand. On the floor was a multitude of small pyramids with sharp edges. To protect his feet, he could only stand between them on his heels or his toes, both positions excruciatingly painful. After a time, Horev fainted.

When he regained consciousness, he remembered being in a most beautiful place, where he was taught, "Never turn your face in anger from your tormentors. Jesus the Master did not turn His face from those who spat on Him. Look at your enemies with the same love with which a bride loves her bridegroom."

Ivan Horev belongs among those lifted to higher spiritual realms.

Soon after this, his son Benjamin Horev was put in the same cell. In it he found an inscription on the wall made by his father. It spoke of loving our enemies.

Every Christian has a cross to bear, but some bear it loving passionately those who impose it on them. They are able to smile at their torturers.

But not all martyrs are like this, since they are on different spiritual levels. Some, primarily those killed for Christ at an early age of their faith, cry out, "How long, 0 Lord, holy and true, until you judge and avenge our blood on those who dwell on the earth?" (Revelation 6:10). Out of caution, God keeps these martyrs under the altar. It would be terrible if such sentiments were to become dominant. But these too have a martyr's crown.

St. Catherine of Siena in the fourteenth century brought to repentance a criminal sentenced to death, whom she had visited in jail. He asked her to be with him when he was beheaded. Early the next morning she went to the place of execution, put her head on the block, and prayed that at the last moment light and peace might be given to him. There is no more effective prayer than that in which you transpose yourself into the situation of the one for whom you pray. The former criminal died with the words "Jesus: Catherine" on his lips and went to the wedding of the Lamb, having been washed in His blood.

We should identify in prayer with the martyrs, especially those who are weak and cannot remain loving and pure to the very end. Pray for them because they too are human and cannot always live on the heights. No ballerina can stand twenty-four hours on tiptoes. No one's behavior is saintly twenty-four hours a day. Even the noblest sufferer for Christ needs comfort, encouragement, and the willingness of a friend to cover up their sins. Even the least among us can be helpful to this extent.

Those who have passed through Communist prisons are unspeakably poor. When arrested, they suffer the loss of home and furniture. Many are no longer able to work physically or

　　　　RICHARD WURMBRAND

intellectually. Their children are not allowed to study or attend school. Therefore they are in desperate need of material help. St. Ambrose said, "Whosoever can help a poor man and does not do so is a thief, and if the other dies of hunger, he is a murderer." Let us be careful. The one from whom we steal or kill in this way may be a Christian who has suffered for his faith.

PART 5

METHODS OF TORTURE

~20~

ONLY FAITH CAN OVERCOME

THE SERBIAN FEMALE LIEUTENANT, VIDAL NEDITCH, specialized in beating men on the genitals with a rod (later she was imprisoned and tortured by her own comrades). Prisoners were given salty food and then kept without water. They were forced to run around their own cells, as in a circus ring, day and night without interruption. Trained dogs would jump at them if they stopped even for a moment. This is how confessions were obtained; these confessions in turn would lead to other sentences.

One torturer, in a moment of relaxation between two sessions of beatings, told his victim that torture was the most ancient of the fine arts, older than love, and certainly much richer and more varied. "Torture is what makes the difference between a man and an animal. Animals can't torture. In the human body, the zones of pleasure are fewer than the zones of pain. Pain is more intense and can last longer than pleasure." This monster believed that if there were a God, He made man to be tortured. "Everything that speeds up the coming of Communism is good. I have no scruples." This torturer ended up in a lunatic asylum.

For hours, prisoners had to listen to lectures about the beauty of the Communist regime. Driven to despair, one prisoner, not wishing to listen any more, cut off his own ears and sent them in a parcel to the Central Committee of the Communist Party. In Romania, a prisoner tattooed on his chest the words "Slave of the Communist Party." For this he was sentenced to death.

A Czech Communist newspaper wrote:

> *The church as a whole has been in prison since 1950. . . . Her press resembles letters from a jail. . . . In prison, guards fired from the observation towers into prison cells, dogs without muzzles were let in the prison hospital, the inmates were beaten on their heads with horsewhips and sprayed with water from hoses, and the investigator yelled: "Do you desire human rights? We do not recognize any humanitarianism."*
>
> *Many of the inmates suffered internal injuries. Some, like Hermanovsky, a very young man, became insane from the torture. In one of the transports was also the 75-year-old bishop Vohtassak. They stripped him naked, and he had to stand for several hours on the stone floor and, when he could not continue the squatting exercises, they yelled at him, "Squat until you spit your soul, you ——————"*

Communists have developed almost irresistible methods of torture. Brigadier-General John Flinn, a prisoner in Vietnam, declared, "They could bring me to a state of mind in which, if they had ordered it, I would have shot my own mother." The United States Government did well to absolve all former prisoners of war of what they said under such extreme duress.

The Albanian prisoner G. Gardin, who served ten years, wrote that on the way to work prisoners passed long blackberry hedges.

One day a young man slowed down to pick some. The guard who followed the line of prisoners found him in the bushes. The marshal was informed, and at dinner time the poor man was hung from the torture-pole, his hands tied with metal wire. At first, he resisted the pain caused by the weight of his body suspended from his wrists. He soon started to yell and implore, "Kill me! . . . Please . . . one shot!" His breathing became difficult and he stopped talking; his face turned purple, and after a while his head bent forward.

Only then did they take him down.

The work-day of prisoners was fifteen hours. Sick prisoners were forced to work until they died of exhaustion. The food ration consisted of a ladle of soup twice a day, two pounds of bread, and meat only once a week. If a prisoner failed to meet the work quota by the end of the day, he received no food in the evening. Sometimes men with no other guilt than pure exhaustion were hung by their feet to a peg and left there for hours head-down. In the heat of summer they were deprived of even a drop of water, just as the damned receive not a drop of water in hell. A Communist jail is its ante-chamber.

The priests Fausti and Dajani were locked for two months in primitive latrines full of excrement. They were then condemned to death, while other Christians were sentenced to life-long imprisonment. When the two priests were led to execution with others, Fausti said, "Let us go to the house of the Lord."

21

UNSPEAKABLE TORTURES

*I*N ROMANIA, UNSPEAKABLE THINGS HAPPENED. D. Bacu reported the following:

> We had to scrub the floors, while two or three other prisoners rode on us. We were obliged to eat like pigs. We had to kneel with our hands handcuffed behind us, and lap hot soup from the dish. At noon, bread was thrown to us, which we had to eat in the same position, using only the mouth. The last crumb had to be gathered from the floor with the lips or tongue. We had to wash the dish with our tongues.
>
> The whole day you had to sit at the bedside, with your feet stretched out, with your hands on your knees, head up, looking straightforward, without the right to move. After sixteen hours of such torture, you were allowed to sleep but only on your back, face upwards, your body perfectly stretched out, with your hands over the blanket. If you changed your position, you were hit powerfully with a stick by the one who watched.

Sixteen prisoners were once put one on top of the other. Under the pressure of this weight, the abdominal muscles of the lowest yielded. He did in the cell what he was not allowed to do in the toilet. He was compelled to clean his underpants with his tongue. At first he refused. Then his fingers were bruised between two pieces of wood. In the end . . .

It was forbidden to hit a prisoner in the temples, in the region of the heart, in the neck, wherever death mightfollow. The Communists did not wish physical death . . . They made a devilish experiment: the death of the soul, to be replaced by conditioned reflexes. Not physical, but moral death.

At Easter, they clothed a prisoner in sheets and made him play the role of Jesus Christ. Out of soap they made a genital organ, which a theological student, the would be Christ, had to wear on his chest instead of the cross. He was forced to walk around the room, beaten with sticks, as if he were on the road to Golgotha. Other Christians had to bow before him, to kiss this genital organ and to say, "I bow before your Almightiness." There was only one who did not stoop to such blasphemy. He was tortured for hours.

The Christian teacher Antonio Borro succeeded in escaping miraculously from Cuba some years ago. Having passed through prison himself, he told how the prisoners were treated. He was put in a cell, a kind of cage, in which he could only sit. He was dragged by the feet to interrogations, during which he was beaten with a rope on his face and with sticks on his back.

Borro was exchanged for some adherents of Castro in Honduras. Otherwise he would have experienced the other tortures applied to prisoners in Cuba. Among them he recounts the following: "Our brethren were bathed in acid; a hammer and sickle were tattooed on the skin with a red hot iron poker; their heads were put in a box of bees." He himself was shown a picture of medical students practicing vivisection on men who

RICHARD WURMBRAND

were still alive, and was threatened with having to undergo this. So he "confessed" to having committed immoral acts, being an agent of the CIA, and an opponent of Communism the last of course being true.

In China, Christians were forced to stand at attention for two hours before a picture of Mao Tse Tung, with three bricks on each shoulder. Every twenty minutes a brick was added. In the end they had to carry eighteen bricks. If their knees buckled for a moment, the torture would begin again. Other Christians had their heads shaved. On the bald head were placed hot ashes, while the victim stood at attention before the idol of Mao.

The Chinese Church has not only survived in spite of these happenings; it has mushroomed. When Mao came to power in 1949, there were 3.5 million Christians in China. After decades of fierce terror, Protestants alone are said to be over 70 million. The number of Catholics has grown, too.

In Vietnam, a number of Buddhist pagodas and churches are kept open in the big cities to preserve appearances, but the majority of the pastors and religious have been sent to concentration camps.

Reverend Thich Quang Do was arrested in 1985. To induce him to collaborate, the Communists also arrested his 85-year-old mother, who was senile. Her hands were so stiff she could no longer hold her bowl, nor could she see to keep herself clean. Thich Quang Do was given the choice of denying his faith or letting his mother perish in suffering and filth.

The world would say, "Do the will of the henchmen and save your mother." But Christians have a "different law." For no reason will they deny the God of Israel, who is the Maker of the universe and the Father of all mankind. He can make a mother's suffering serve her eternal good.

Mordecai's refusal to bow to the tyrant Haman—as recounted in the biblical book of Esther—threatened the existence of the whole Jewish nation, yet he did not bow, and God saved the nation. Haman and his ten sons, who were like him, were hanged.

The Communists trained male and female Secret Police officers to be professional seducers. They sent them to Christian prisoners, who many times had been doped with sexually-stimulating drugs beforehand, to seduce them. The moment the victim had fallen into their net, a snapshot was taken. Then the victim was blackmailed: "If we publish the picture, your family and your church will despise you." Some were asked afterwards to become informers of the Secret Police or were forced to give public statements that they denied Christ.

Mary X was an outstanding example of faith. Judged together with Tchernetskaia for having run secret Sunday schools, she had been sentenced to four years of prison, while Tchernetskaia was sentenced to five. Mary protested against the milder sentence, asking for the privilege of suffering as much as her friend. But towards the end of her sentence a professional seducer was sent to her. She fell into sin and under blackmail gave a shameful declaration denying her faith.

Similar things happen with brethren after they have passed through many years of prison. In the Old Testament, Joseph refused the temptation of a beautiful woman. Many others have done the same, but they had not been administered mind-bending drugs as is the case with our sisters and brethren, and their nerves were not shattered through brainwashing and torture.

Leaders of the Underground Church whom we met told us, with tears in their eyes, "We knew how to resist atheist propaganda and torture, but we did not know how to counteract the forced drugging."

There always remains a solution: What one can't resist should be borne in faith as another cross of strange design. Love bears all things—all, without exception. It also bears inescapable sins.

~22~

Mind-Bending Drugs

*I*N VIETNAM, A NUMBER OF BUDDHIST PAGODAS and churches are kept open in the big cities to preserve appearances, but the majority of the pastors and religious have been sent to concentration camps.

Reverend Thich Quang Do was arrested in 1985. To induce him to collaborate, the Communists also arrested his 85-year-old mother, who was senile. Her hands were so stiff she could no longer hold her bowl, nor could she see to keep herself clean. Thich Quang Do was given the choice of denying his faith or letting his mother perish in suffering and filth.

The same methods are used against many Buddhists.

The world would say, "Do the will of the henchmen and save your mother." But Christians have a "different law." For no reason will they deny the God of Israel, who is the Maker of the universe and the Father of all mankind. He can make a mother's suffering serve her eternal good.

Mordecai's refusal to bow to the tyrant Haman-as recounted in the biblical book of Esther-threatened the existence of the whole Jewish nation, yet he did not bow, and God saved the nation. Haman and his ten sons, who were like him, were hanged.

The Communists trained male and female Secret Police officers to be professional seducers. They sent them to Christian prisoners, who many times had been doped with sexually-stimulating drugs beforehand, to seduce them. The moment the victim had fallen into their net, a snapshot was taken. Then the victim was blackmailed: "If we publish the picture, your family and your church will despise you." Some were asked afterwards to become informers of the Secret Police or were forced to give public statements that they denied Christ.

Mary X was an outstanding example of faith. Judged together with Tchernetskaia for having run secret Sunday schools, she had been sentenced to four years of prison, while Tchernetskaia was sentenced to five. Mary protested against the milder sentence, asking for the privilege of suffering as much as her friend. But towards the end of her sentence a professional seducer was sent to her. She fell into sin and under blackmail gave a shameful declaration denying her faith.

Similar things happen with brethren after they have passed through many years of prison. In the Old Testament, Joseph refused the temptation of a beautiful woman. Many others have done the same, but they had not been administered mind-bending drugs as is the case with our sisters and brethren, and their nerves were not shattered through brainwashing and torture.

Leaders of the Underground Church whom we met told us, with tears in their eyes, "We knew how to resist atheist propaganda and torture, but we did not know how to counteract the forced drugging."

There always remains a solution: What one can't resist should be borne in faith as another cross of strange design. Love bears all things-all, without exception. It also bears inescapable sins.

23

WHAT FALSE CHURCH LEADERS PRAISED

OUR HEART ACHES FOR THE LEADERS OF ALL official denominations in the former USSR. They, along with those who worked with them in the West, praised religious liberty under Communism, which did not exist. To show what these men praised, I quote from the book *Let History Judge*, by the Russian Communist, Roy Medvedev. The source cannot be challenged. In this work he tells some of the tortures applied to prisoners in the Leninist jails of the Soviet Union. Among them were innumerable Christians. Children were killed in the presence of their mothers to make the mother confess to imaginary crimes. When one prisoner refused to denounce innocents, a person completely unknown to him was brought in. The prisoner was told, "He will be shot if you do not sign what we ask." Thinking it a joke, the prisoner refused. The man was shot. After a few days, a second youngster was shot before his eyes. To avoid the killing of others, the prisoner then denounced his friends, who afterwards were also killed. The prisoner never recovered, knowing himself to be guilty of the death of many.

The Communists gouged out the eyes of prisoners and perforated eardrums. They put out their cigarettes on the naked bodies of prisoners and ripped open stomachs. In Leningrad, prisoners were covered by a box with nails driven in from all four sides. Others were forced to drink urine. Medvedev, himself a Leninist and a partisan of terror, criticized only what he called "excess." A Communist exposed Communist cruelty.

Official church leaders praised the one who initiated it. At the same time, they called the brethren of the Underground Church, "the devil's fire."

We should not swallow the lie that there was terror only in Stalin's day. His successors were equally guilty. It seems that the extent of their crimes becomes known only after their downfall. Tortures like those described above might have broken our sister Mary X, who was sentenced to five years of prison for her faith. In a Communist newspaper she acknowledged that she had been imprisoned justly because she had really committed the crime of teaching children about Christ. She asked people abroad not to bother about her but to take up the defense of Angela Davis, the American Communist charged with the murder of four people. She finished her article with the words, "I ask parents and educators to warn their children about men of the Church and of the sects."

How much urine were Christian girls compelled to drink before writing such things? Were their mothers beaten in their presence? They were weak. A Christian should fear nothing except God and fear. But a church leader who praises Lenin, the initiator of this system, is a disgrace. And church leaders who praise the one who praised Lenin are another disgrace.

Bishop Marshall of the Lutheran Church of America wrote sympathetically about his meeting with the Lutheran bishop of Hungary, Kaldy, a man whom he described as "enthusiastic about the Communist economic and political system." Enthusiastic about the political system that kept in prison the pastors Hegyeman, Turi, Katona, and many other Christians? Enthusiastic about a system imposed on Hungary by Russian tanks? A system that forbade pastors any contact with youth?

RICHARD WURMBRAND

Bishops should be "lovers of good," not of regimes that torture and poison children with atheism.

There are faithful bishops who give their lives for the Church. There are other men of high rank in the Church who are not "lovers of good." Be very careful to whom you entrust your soul. God gave some to be pastors and teachers "for the perfecting of the saints," to make them grow "unto the measure of the stature of the fullness of Christ" (Ephesians 4:11–13). A bishop or pastor should lead you to high fellowship with God. If he does not, find someone better.

If you have been unsuccessful in finding the right pastor in your community, take the faithful pastors of the Underground Church as your example. Prayer will unite you with them. You will catch their fire; and you will set your church on fire.

Somewhere a church was burning down. Among the spectators was a well-known atheist. The pastor said to him, "While the church was in good condition, you did not attend. But now that it is on fire, you come."

The atheist replied, "If your church had always been on fire, I would have attended regularly."

PART 6

FALLING AND RISING AGAIN

24

RAPED MINDS

*J*ESUS WOULD NOT ENTER THE HOUSE OF A DISCIPLE if not invited. The Communists, on the other hand, use even the threat of homosexual rape to subdue the minds of believers. For this purpose they put the brethren Klassen and Tchemodanov in cells reserved for homosexuals.

They forced the Orthodox priest Dudko to recant on nationwide television. Dudko had been the most renowned evangelist of the USSR. Solzhenitsyn and other prominent Russian personalities consider him their spiritual father. But under threat, he expressed his regret for his "fight against atheism, which is a fight against the Soviet regime." He acknowledged that he had done great harm to the church and the country by his preaching.

We feel that Dudko is not guilty before God. One who is injected with depersonalizing chemical substances or subjected to extreme beatings and pressure is no longer himself and is thus not responsible for his actions. Jesus never steps across the threshold of our will, but asks for our consent, as we should do to others. By contrast, Communist leaders impose their will with cruelty.

When the situation changed in the USSR, Dudko wrote in a new book, *The Lost Coin*: "I realize that in prison I have betrayed the interests of the Church. I have in my soul inexpressible pain. I see no way out. I am ready to do anything to repair my fault. How did I come to such a point? This question gives me no peace day or night."

In a letter he says, "I overestimated my resources, and no one has ever fallen so low. Why? What happened? Whom should I accuse? First, surely, myself."

The hope for Dudko, as for all of us, is the finished work of Christ. On the cross, Jesus said, "It is finished" (John 19:30). He had made perfect expiation for sin, satisfying all the demands of the law. He has paid all our debts. There remains nothing for us to do, however low we may have fallen, except to receive His love with confidence and to continue our life with praise. Though one is abandoned by all others, they are not abandoned by God.

Such are also counted heroes before God. Their temporary fall is not imputed to them. The apostle Peter, called "the rock" by Jesus, fell repeatedly into sin. The other apostles fled when Jesus was arrested.

Let us also walk the way of heroism, though we live under entirely different circumstances. Let us do so even with stumbling steps. If we fall seven times in a day, we can be forgiven. We are considered by God as if we had never sinned.

~25~

BE GRAND AMONG DWARFS

CHRIST INVITES EVERYONE TO GRANDEUR. IF ONE cannot be even the smallest of the giants, he can strive to be the greatest among dwarfs.

A Romanian Orthodox priest, whom we'll call X, had been an anti-Semite and had written a book proving that a Jew cannot become a Christian. Soon after the Communist takeover, he changed his politics and became a collaborator with the Reds. He won their confidence and was given a high position in the Ministry of Cults.

Later he became converted. He remained in favor with the Communists and so could reveal to us their secrets, including the names of informers within the church—he even told us those who had informed against me. He rendered the Underground Church important services while making a semblance of being loyal to the Reds. At the congress of the World Council of Churches in Uppsala, he spoke publicly against us, but secretly he met with leaders of our Scandinavian missions and assured them that the assertions about the persecutions were correct and all accusations brought against me were slander.

We honor his memory. God will reward him for the good done to the Underground Church, though it would certainly be much better if there were no compromise at all, if every Christian would say a decided "no" to every temptation of sin or fear.

We cannot, however, point an accusing finger at those who are less heroic than others. Sometimes it is easy to be courageous; sometimes it is most difficult.

To those who served God with their weakness, I quote the words of Jesus: "All cannot receive this saying, save they to whom it is given" (Matthew 19:11). These words have freed my conscience from many unfounded regrets and much painful remorse. They can free others, too.

It is obvious that not all commandments of the Bible are written for all believers. No one is obliged to fulfill all of them, and we must not feel bad when we cannot accomplish them. Some commandments are given only to the Jewish priests, others only to husbands or wives, others to children. The commandments for masters are not the same as those to servants. Many verses concern exclusively the generation that conquered Canaan. Some apply only to farmers. God does not expect the same thing from those of various temperaments and different educational backgrounds.

Everyone should serve God according to their calling and their own gifts, without torturing their conscience over the fact that they cannot do other things for which they are not qualified. Many of those who were heroes in the encounter with Communist terror and suffered much, once freed, showed no power at all to resist the temptations of sex, money, or pride.

As one body, all together, we should fulfill the whole law, but no individual alone can be expected to fulfill it. Only Jesus was able to say, "I came to fulfil the law" (Matthew 5:17).

There are certain commands that can be received only by exceptional beings to whom they are given and only in corresponding situations.

Whatever kind of persons we are, let us strive to be at least grand dwarfs.

RICHARD WURMBRAND

26

COMPROMISE AND REGRET

*I*N ROMANIA, WHEN A NUN WHO HAD BEEN IN hiding was arrested, she cracked under torture and gave the names of all who had sheltered her and even those who had ever given her something to eat. They were all given life sentences, and their whole families were arrested, including grandparents, parents, and children. Many died. The nun passed her days weeping about what she had done.

An Italian paper told the story of a bishop who returned to his cell from an interrogation under torture, no longer recognizing his friends. He repeated again and again, "I have no other alternative but to hang myself." He was a man of fifty who had been active, capable, courageous.

At the World Baptist Congress in Tokyo, the Soviet delegation lied about religious liberty in their country and paraded the blood-stained flag of Communism along with the flags of the other nations represented. I stood up and protested loudly: "This is not the flag of Russia, but the universal flag of God-hatred. It is red with the blood of the martyrs." Some Baptists used physical violence to drive me out of the Congress, as 10,000 delegates from countries worldwide cheered the Red flag. Not one took up my defense.

But the story does not end there. When I went to the Baptist church in Moscow in 1991, Bytchkov (who had been their General Secretary) kissed me and said publicly, "Fascists and Communists have beaten you. We Baptists have beaten you, too." How many preachers who have not sinned like the Russian Baptist collaborators of Communism would have exhibited the heroism of such a humble apology? How many of those who have not sinned like the bishop or nun would have repented, as Jesus said, "in sackcloth and ashes"?

Today we should be slow to condemn believers who, under pressure, did foolish things. We must keep in mind how much they have suffered. In Czechoslovakia, the Communists put an empty bucket over the head of a bound prisoner and hammered on it again and again. Laughing contemptuously, they said, "By this method we could make even Jesus say He is not the Savior."

They were wrong about Jesus. But humans are often very weak and sometimes yield to more than physical tortures.

Iurii Shukevitch was imprisoned as a child for his father's "crime" of being a Ukrainian fighter against Communism. When asked to dissociate himself from his father, he refused, just as my wife and son did when I was thrown into Romanian jails. Shukevitch was in jail and deported for thirty-four years (1948–1968 and 1972–1986) for fulfilling the one commandment with a promised blessing: "Honor your parents." Then after he became blind and had gone through all that suffering, he had even greater pain inflicted upon him: the Communists published a forged letter in which he allegedly denied his father.

Individuals whose childhoods were stolen from them, who are heroes of the faith, are often victims of depression. They are prone to irrational attitudes and aggressiveness, even against friends. Their whole life becomes distorted, even if they are Christians, because in jail they had no opportunity to learn more Christian doctrine.

It is written in Revelation 4:8 that certain heavenly beings are covered with eyes. Therefore they perhaps see not only what we do and the conditions that shaped our actions, but also what we would have been under different circumstances. No violinist

RICHARD WURMBRAND

can play without a violin. Can God's wisdom penetrate a brain damaged by torture? One bishop betrayed friends and then regretted it. Under the influence of drugs, a bishop declared, contrary to his convictions, "The Vatican is an international center of espionage led by warmongers."

Jesus called Judas, after Judas had betrayed Him without any pressure to do so, "friend." Will He not do the same to this nun, this bishop, to you and me when we give way to impulses stronger than our consciences? If this nun and the bishop had lived in a free country, they might have been model Christians.

Solzhenitsyn, the Christian writer and Nobel prize winner expelled from the Soviet Union, states that in the first thirty-five years of the Communist regime between forty and fifty million citizens passed through concentration camps, and more followed later. But these are not the only victims of Communism. How many millions have become Judases to save their own liberty by causing others to enter prison? How many yielded to the tragedy of becoming torturers and inhumane guards? The faith of how many other millions has been destroyed, because they were not able to bear seeing so much suffering in a world created by a loving God?

~27~

RISING AFTER A DEEP FALL

A T LEAST 50,000 ORTHODOX PRIESTS WERE killed by the Soviets. An Orthodox priest, Father Mihail, was among the few not yet arrested, but he had lost his faith. The loss came suddenly. He had just chanted during the liturgy "Blessed be God" when he heard a voice whispering, "There is no God."

He looked questioningly at the images of saints hanging on the walls. What did their friendship with God mean? Does such a mighty Friend allow His believers to be thrown before wild beasts, burned on stakes, tortured inhumanely? He tried to repress these thoughts. He repeated to himself again and again the words of the psalm, "The fool has said in his heart, There is no God." It did not help.

Subsequent to that moment, he continued to act as a priest out of a sense of duty, but he no longer believed. The sorrow around him was too great. He had to restrain himself to keep from crying out to the peasants who filled the church, "Go home, poor people. There is no God. God, if He existed, would not permit this bloody chaos."

Drunken Communists arrested him on an Easter eve. Among them was the cantor of his church, whom he had dismissed because of immoral behavior. Now he too was a Communist. The head of the gang told the priest, "We have decided to kill you. What have you to say?"

Life was worthless for Father Mihail. He answered, "As you like."

But he was given a chance: "If you renounce Christ and trample on a cross, you will be freed."

The thought passed through his mind, "I don't believe. What does a cross mean to me? Let me save my life." But when he opened his mouth, he said, to his own surprise, "I believe in one God."

Then the former cantor proposed that he should be crucified. "It is Easter," he said, "Let him be resurrected." As a caricature of the crown of thorns, they put Mihail's fur cap on his head with the linen on the outside, and they put a sack upon his shoulders as a royal garment. When they finished, the cantor knelt in front of him and said, "Hail, King of the Jews!" Then they beat him.

He prayed to the One in whom he did not believe: "If You exist, save me." With a loud voice, he repeated, "I believe in one God."

This made such an impression upon the drunken murderers that they freed him. He came home, prostrated himself on the earth in his prayer corner, and said with tears, "I believe."

By being faithful in spite of extreme doubts, by asserting his belief when dark clouds had separated him from heaven, by sharing the suffering of Christ though he was not even sure any more of His existence, Father Mihail won his soul.

Some Christians bear their suffering with patience, resignation, and love. Other martyrs ask the torturers who insult and mistreat them to forgive them for not having been even better Christians. A believer once wrote, "The first five years in jail I suffered as an innocent. When I reached the twentieth year, I realized my guilt. Everyone is guilty who has been less than a son, less than Christlike."

$\mathscr{28}$

SMALL GEMS

$\mathcal{G}$ENUINE HEROES, LARGER-THAN-LIFE FIGURES, ARE rare. Heroes are persons for whom the exceptional becomes the norm. Frequently they do not last long. Some of them might not have ended up as heroes if they had lived longer. But there are little gems even among those who tried and did not succeed. More souls have been won for Christ by preachers who did what little they could, than by renowned evangelists.

A tiny poodle once stood near a wolfhound. The large dog asked scornfully, "Do you consider yourself a dog?"

The little one did not have the courage to stand up to the large dog but nevertheless replied, "Sir, I might not be such a big dog as you, but neither can you say I am a cat."

The smallest dog is still a dog. And a person who shows a little bit of heroism in Christian life is still a hero. But there are some who called themselves Christians who showed no heroism at all. Many of the top leaders of the official Baptist Church in the former Soviet Union were stooges of the Communists. Here is a letter of instruction issued by the leadership to the churches in 1960. It was written by the Baptist pastor Karev:

The young under 18 should not be baptized. Baptisms of persons between 18 and 30 have to be reduced to a minimum. Gatherings of pastors are forbidden, as are courses for teaching music directors, and the gathering of funds for the poor. Pastors have to take a stand against missionary activities, since they are "unhealthy."

Such instructions were given not by atheist authorities directly but by Baptist preachers who had become their servants. The rank-and-file Christian knew that his pastor was a traitor. But in the show church in Moscow this same pastor had to read from the Bible. The songs praised the Savior. The sermon, though not delivered in the right spirit, mentioned the name of Jesus. What a mighty work of God it was that thousands of Christians did not take offense at the wicked character of their pastor but thronged the church to hear the name of Christ and to adore Him. One can worship God even in a religious service led by a Judas. This same thing happened in the Soviet Orthodox Church. The Christian Nobel prize winner Alexander Solzhenitsyn revealed that the synod of bishops was guided by the Communist state. He wrote:

A church led in a dictatorial manner by atheists is something unheard of in almost 2,000 years of Christianity. The . printed Gospel can be obtained nowhere in our country. We receive the Bible from abroad [a reference to organizations like ours that smuggle Bibles]. But Orthodox believers pack the churches in which the liturgy is said by bishops and priests who are tools of Communism. The traitors chant the praises of Christ. They give a communion which is so holy that not even its being consecrated and imparted by a treacherous priest makes it lose its value.

Not all preachers who do such things are stooges. Some are real Christians who try to serve their Master in this shameful way. There exists not only the spoken word but also body language—the gestures, facial expressions, and tears running down the cheeks.

In Japanese there are forty words for "No." Some of them mean "yes."

I knew a man who had to laud the Communist regime in his speech. These were his words: "Under the wise leadership of the genial Ceausescu and the Communist Party, our country is lifted yearly to a higher and higher way of life, up to the zenith." But as he pronounced these words, he began with his arms lifted high. Every time he said the word "higher" he lowered his arms a little bit more. When he said "zenith" his arms were at his side.

Everyone understood what he meant. This is also a way to express the truth.

That man ended up in prison, but he had served the truth in his own way. There had been a spark of heroism in him.

PART 7
HIGHER GROUND

~29~

PREPARE TO ENTER THROUGH THE VEIL

THERE IS A SPECIAL MANNER OF WORSHIPING GOD—
it involves action.

A man dug weeds together with his wife in their garden. Looking up, he saw an angel, who said to him, "It is time to come to your eternal abode."

The man answered, "It would leave so much more work for my wife to do. Please allow me to finish." The angel nodded his assent.

In the evening, the man helped his wife wash the dishes. The angel came again, calling him to the eternal abode. But they had had guests and the dishes were many. The man said, "I don't want to leave the whole burden of putting the house in order to my wife. Please let me tarry a little bit longer." Again the angel agreed.

Later, when the man had gone to bed, he called the angel and said, "Now you can come and take me to the eternal abode."

The angel appeared and said, "That is where you have been this whole day."

To work for the Kingdom of heaven is heaven. To work for the glory of God is to worship. God calls Christians to be active in his harvest.

"Ye become followers of us and of the Lord" (1 Thessalonians 1:6). St. Paul considered himself the chief of sinners. He surely did not lie when he referred to himself this way, nor did he display false humility. He must have had serious motives to describe himself like this. Notwithstanding, he was sure that whoever followed him and his co-workers became by this very fact also a follower of Christ. He had this confidence in his calling.

~30~

A LANGUAGE WITHOUT THE WORDS "TO HAVE"

*L*UKE RECORDS THAT "THERE WAS A CERTAIN RICH man which had . . . " (16:1), and "A certain man had . . . " (15:11).

The Bible is God's revelation. Revelation is a word of Latin origin that has two meanings. It discovers hidden things unknown before, but it also reveils them—it puts them behind a veil. From the beginning, the words of our Lord were conveyed to us in Greek, a language other than that spoken by Jesus. We have His words in the veil of a translation, which can never convey the full sense of the original, and even the Hebrew of the Old Testament veils the thoughts of God, wrapping them in the poor language of men. The purpose of the Bible is to awaken in us a longing for the blessed state when there was no Creator and no creation, when there was only God and we were all in Him; when there was no communication among men in words unfit to express the highest thoughts, and we were one in Him; as it will be again at the consummation of the ages.

Jesus spoke Aramaic, a dialect of the Hebrew language. Neither in Aramaic nor in Hebrew does the word "to have" exist. So Jesus never pronounced this word. Jesus never said about anything that He "had" it. Therefore He could retain perfect joy when He was undressed to be scourged, since He had never said about His clothes, "I have them."

He had never said, "I have a body." The body that was tortured was not His. He owned nothing. He had yielded His body to His Father as a living sacrifice before being killed. He never said, "I have a mother." As you cannot be separated from what you don't have, He did not feel death as a separation from her.

He taught His first disciples to think in the same manner. "Neither said any of them that any of the things which he possessed was his own" (Acts 4:32). Everything belongs to God and we are the stewards of His possessions. He is free to take away at any time the material riches, health, a beloved child, a good name, a friend, fame. These things are only entrusted to us. If they are taken away we lose nothing. They are not ours.

This constitutes one of the joys of the Christian life. All Christians are "have-nots" and do not desire to be "haves." Those who have, worry about possible losses. This is not possible for us. Our life is one of full serenity.

In his book, *The Release of the Spirit*, Watchman Nee, who died in a Chinese jail, took this thought the furthest when he wrote, "If we have to remember to pray, this shows that our outer man has not been broken; for if it were, unceasing communion with the Lord would exist."

Christians do not have a Lord, because this implies one other than them. Christians are one with the Lord, a part of His mystical body.

Having nothing of our own, but being one with the compassionate Lord, we look with His eyes upon this troubled world.

RICHARD WURMBRAND

~31~

PARABLE OF THE THREE TREES

*I*N UNDERGROUND CHURCHES THE PARABLE OF THE three trees is often told. It also comforts prisoners of faith. We think it is useful for children and adults in the West as well.

In a forest, the story goes, three young trees were great friends. They all agreed to pray not to die by decaying in old age, but to be felled so that their wood might be useful to men.

The first tree desired to become a manger in which tired cattle would feed after a long day's work. God rewarded its modesty. It became a very special manger—the one in which was laid the very Son of God. It saw the angels watching over the Child. It heard the blessed virgin's lullabies. Wise men and shepherds bowed before it. What tree had ever had a more beautiful fate?

The second tree, looking at the boats on the lake below, prayed that its wood might be used for making a boat. The prayer was answered, and many travelers embarked and disembarked as they went about their business. On a particular day it had a special passenger: the Son of God. It heard Jesus speak words of love and wisdom never known before. In a fierce storm, it seemed that the boat would perish, but He said,

"Peace, be still!" and the tempest stopped immediately. It had been worthwhile to die as a tree to witness such a scene.

The third tree did not know what it wanted to be, so others decided for it. They made out of it a large cross to serve as an instrument of torture. Who was ever sadder than this tree? One day the Son of God was nailed to it. But the Cross did not hear groaning and swearing as on other crosses. It heard words of divine forgiveness, words opening the gates of heaven even to a repenting thief, caring words for His mother, and words of confidence to His Father. The wood then understood that its part in the crucifixion of Jesus provided for the salvation of mankind.

We also rejoice about our crosses and tribulations.

Ordinarily, no one seeks pain. Only exceptional souls are called to great renunciation: voluntary poverty, chastity, obedience, even unto death. We others do not rejoice because of tribulations. We could well go on without them, yet we rejoice in them at least if they cannot be avoided.

Tribulations can also be a source of happiness and peace.

~32~

SERVING ALL YOUR DAYS

*J*UST AS YOU HAVE TO OVERCOME THE DIFFICULTIES of beginning, so you must resist the temptation to finish your work before the last breath. God can enable you to serve Him all the days of your life, right to the end.

To abandon the cause at an age when one has accumulated valuable experience is selfish. Getting old does not necessarily mean becoming weak. The Greek dramatist Sophocles wrote Oedipus at the age of ninety. Titian painted at ninety-nine, as did the Russian painter Repin at eighty-six. Verdi wrote his last opera at the age of eighty. "When Isaac was old, his eyes were dim" (Genesis 27:1). "Eli was ninety and eight years old; and his eyes were dim" (1 Samuel 4:15). Moses was 120 and his eyes were not dim. He could lead his people to the very end, and before his death he delivered important speeches that have guided the faithful for thousands of years. It is because Moses was privileged to see God face to face. But we too may have this privilege, which enables us to be useful in His kingdom whatever our age or outward condition.

The blessings we hear in church: "The Lord make His face to shine upon you" and "the Lord lift up His countenance upon you" (Numbers 6:25–26), would be meaningless if we could not see God's face. In Jesus, God became real and visible. I can evoke His face before my eyes just like the face of anyone else dear to me. Knowing how my wife relates to me, I can be sure of her expression if I wish to "see" her in my mind's eye. So also can I see the face of God in relation to me.

A courier of our mission found an Underground Church in China whose pastor was 103. He had not retired at seventy, nor at eighty or ninety. Why then should he retire at 103? He lived in a hut with no furniture but a straw mattress. He was a successful pastor, with as many disciples as Jesus: twelve were gathered in his home.

~33~

BEGIN WITH LITTLE THINGS

THE THOUGHT MIGHT OCCUR TO YOU: "THE height to which this book calls me is not for me." This then would also be your reply to Jesus' call, "Be ye therefore perfect, even as your Father which is in heaven is perfect" (Matthew 5:48). I have invented nothing. The challenge I gave is from Jesus.

But perhaps there is still a misunderstanding.

Let us suppose you have a child in elementary school who is a perfect pupil. His penmanship is beautiful, and he writes as he is taught. He gets all A's. He is perfect for his age. Later he can be a perfect son, a perfect teenager, a perfect college student. There are stages in perfection.

Ascent toward heaven's perfection starts with a descent, with a split in a man's consciousness. He realizes that he is constituted of two persons. God calls "Abraham, Abraham" (Genesis 22:11), "Samuel, Samuel" (1 Samuel 3:10), with a line between the two names called a disjunctive sign, showing separation. It could be translated "the two persons living in Abraham." You are at the same time what you are and what you must become. You are a fact and an ideal. You are a chaos and an incipient cosmos. You are a compound of vague desires and firm decisions.

The fight begins within yourself to become a harmonious personality, a fulfillment of the ideal. When God says "Moses, Moses," there is no more a disjunctive sign. The two sides serve the Lord. This is the fulfillment of the commandment, "You shall love the Lord your God with all your heart" (Luke 10:27).

Nowadays one can be a church-goer all his life and never hear a word about mortification, though the Bible recommends it, just as it teaches that salvation is by faith. "Mortify your members," says the apostle Paul.

Practice humility, which Vincent de Paul calls the most powerful weapon to overcome the devil, because he neither knows how to use it nor does he understand how to defend himself against it.

Deny yourself in little things to learn the great denial: the denial of the self.

Don't complain about your crosses. By the very fact that we call our sufferings crosses, we acknowledge their holiness. Receive them with great affection.

Give evidence of meekness through your words, gestures, actions.

Give up commanding and start obeying in all matters except sin.

Be simple like little children who think, speak, and act sincerely.

Don't lose time. Bonaventure said that one loses glory in proportion to the number of good deeds he could have done in that hour.

Use more and more of your time in prayer.

Believing that God is omnipotent, wise and good, have full confidence in Him.

Love and love some more. Choose this above every other attitude. God knows how weak we are, and appreciates good intentions that we are too weak to fulfill as if they were good deeds.

~34~

Don't Believe Only in a Historic Christ

OT ALL CHRISTIANS THINK ALIKE. SOME believe that Christ was born only in Bethlehem for our salvation, and they celebrate this event at Christmas. Others, rejecting the spiritual contraceptives of unbelief and pride, have allowed Christ to be born also in their own souls after being touched by the Holy Spirit. Furthermore, they have kept worldliness and false teaching from bringing the Divine embryo to abortion. He lives within their hearts.

When Michelangelo used a stone-mason as a model for a statue of Christ, he was criticized by his teacher Ghirlandio. Michelangelo defended himself: "But Christ was also a workingman, a carpenter."

The master replied, "Florence won't accept a workingclass Christ. They are used to having Him as a nobleman."

So some are accustomed only to a historical Savior. They would not accept an inner Christ—even though to be real, Christ must dwell within the heart. To all outward appearances, Jesus was a Jewish carpenter and rabbi. Thousands knew Him without observing that He was more. His being Christ became visible only through spiritual insight.

Thus it is today. I invite you to take a step forward from celebrating only Jesus' birth in Bethlehem two thousand years ago. We must become Christian "in the inward parts" (Psalm 51:6).

A Christmas focusing only on the outward, historical event is perilous to the soul. It brings death in the disguise of merriment, whereas Christ born within brings life eternal. Once Christ lives in us, we are "the light of the world" and "the salt of the earth" (Matthew 5:13–14), "partakers of the divine nature" (2 Peter 1:4), children of God. Then we can rejoice about, and in spite of, everything. When the sea becomes stormy, fish descend to the depths where it is calm. When suffering and disappointment of all kinds accumulate in your life, add to them the suffering of others. With Christ, enter into the depths of even greater sorrows freely chosen. Go willingly to Gethsemane!

We are told only once that Jesus and His disciples sang. It was just after the Last Supper, when He went to Gethsemane to be betrayed, forsaken, bound, and delivered into the hands of murderers. "Rejoice!" He says. Deep joy is the privilege of those who, prompted by love, choose heavy crosses. Jesus sang a psalm of praise knowing that, in addition to dying on a cross for us, according to a prophecy, He would bear a suffering not prophesied: descending into hell. Out of the depths of our being He communicates this joy to us. Add to your suffering the weeping with those who weep. This will give you joy.

We can rejoice because there are Christians like the Russian, Mary Avinova, who told her Communist interrogators, "I believe in God, in truth, nobility and beauty, and I hope to do so until I die. I don't fear the sufferings you impose upon me. Dostoyevsky once said, 'Where there is sorrow and pain, the soil is sacred.'"

She was in jail not only with fellow Christians and criminals but also with Communists who had some quarrel with their Party and were now sentenced. One of them, a woman, told Mary: "I have one son. I wanted to make him a first-class Communist, but he was too soft-hearted. So I got together two dozen puppies and kittens in a basket and ordered him to drown them. He burst into tears, but I made him do it. He had to be a ruthless fighter for Communism. We know no pity, compassion, or other bourgeois weaknesses." Her son now tortured his own mother and Mary without compunction.

But this picture is not all dark. There is reason to rejoice. Avinova was able to give comfort and light and eternal hope to this monstrous mother who had made such a son.

~35~

CHILDREN OF PROMISE

THE APOSTLE PAUL WROTE TO THE ROMANS, "THEY which are the children of the flesh, these are not the children of God: but the children of the promise are counted for the seed. For this is the word of promise, At this time will I come, and Sarah shall have a son" (Romans 9:89).

The Bible divides people into two categories: the children of the flesh, who have been born naturally and live the usual way in the world, and the children of promise, who are born-again by a miracle of God and live, on this earth, the holy life expected of citizens in the promised land of heaven.

Isaac is the first person in the Bible called a "child of promise." His life is an example for us. Children of promise have a good conscience, which keeps them from killing someone or even hurting their reputation or wellbeing.

Don't add to your suffering the futile exercise of trying to find out its cause. When Isaac was still young and could not possibly understand what was happening, his father Abraham bound him and lifted his knife to kill him (Genesis 22). When his life was saved, he did not say a word of reproach to his father, nor did he question him. He continued to love and respect his father until he could understand more fully what had happened.

Later a servant of his father decided on his behalf who would be his wife. He did not insist upon his right to choose for himself. The servant had chosen Rebekah, and "he loved her" (Genesis 24:67). He would have loved any other girl an old servant might have picked for him.

When Isaac dug a well of water, other men contended, "The well is ours." Isaac did not go to court. He left them the well and dug another. When that too was taken over by herdsmen, without a word of quarrel he dug a third, until he had satisfied all his covetous neighbors with wells. In the end he had one for himself. When his son Jacob cheated him, he uttered no word of reproach. "Isaac called Jacob and blessed him" (Genesis 28:1).

Accept quietly what God gives you that is as yet unintelligible, and do not fear. Do not fear even torture. Christians are under no obligation to be in their bodies while being tortured. Paul wrote about a man caught up to the third heaven, "whether in the body, I cannot tell; or whether out of the body, I cannot tell" (2 Corinthians 12:2). If you learn to dwell out of the body, even the wrongs in your life are no longer committed by you but by the sin that dwells in you (Romans 7:17). The daily afflictions and even tortures do not make you lose your inner peace.

~36~

Your Life Can Be Exemplary

And the Lord God prepared a gourd and made it to come up over Jonah that it might be a shadow over his head . . . So Jonah was exceeding glad of the gourd" *(Jonah 4:6).*

*I*N THE BIBLE THE SHADOW IS AN IMAGE OF THE transitory. "Our days on earth are a shadow," says Bildad (Job 8:9). "Man flees as a shadow and continues not," says Job himself (14:2). "Man spends all the days of his vain life as a shadow," says Solomon (Ecclesiastes 6:12). He had inherited this thought from his father David. "Our days on the earth are as a shadow and there is none abiding" (1 Chronicles 29:5).

Even prophets like Jonah are sometimes "exceedingly glad" about what is very transitory. He had first made a booth so he could sit under its shadow, forgetting that whatever a man constructs is transitory. A vehement wind overthrew the booth the next day. There is nothing that we construct for ourselves that will not be destroyed. Nothing lasts forever, not even civilizations, let alone us as individuals on this earth.

Jonah was exceedingly glad because of the shadow given by a gourd. But the next day a worm "smote it." Every gourd dies some day, as well as the worm that has eaten it and the prophet who sat under its shadow. Nineveh, to whom Jonah preached, also passed away, though it was granted another century and a half after its repentance. Believers die, as do unbelievers.

There is no sense in being exceedingly glad because of a shadow. Tomorrow you will wish to die because you lost this joy. But the despair will not last because it too is transitory like every feeling. Then the earth on which the gourd grew, about which men were sometimes glad and sometimes angry, will also burn. Only God is everlasting, and it was He who said, "Should I not spare?" (Jonah 4:11). Nineveh He would not spare forever. Even Lazarus, whom Jesus resurrected, had to die again. Only God lives forever. And His word remains: "Shall I not spare?" Shall I not spare in eternity the soul that has trusted in Me?

Christians don't seek their comfort in the shadow of what passes. They are not depressed because of defeats and failures—victories might follow. They are not inebriated by successes. These too do not last. They have an unvarying source of joy—their eternal Lord, who will share eternity with them.

According to the law of gravity, all objects are attracted toward the center of the earth. But flowers grow upward and planes rise to high altitudes, not because the law of gravity is false, but because gravity is not the only law. Biological laws are at work in the case of the flower, laws of aerodynamics in the case of the plane. There are forces in nature that overcome the force of gravity.

Psychology would say that the result of prolonged persecution united with betrayal on the part of some Church leaders who weaken the faith can only wear out the saints. But this depressive force is not the only one. It is counteracted by the power of the Holy Spirit and by the communion of the saints. Paul, writing to Timothy, gives himself as an example: "Thou hast fully known my doctrine, manner of life, purpose, faith, long-suffering, charity, patience" (2 Timothy 3:10). Modern

RICHARD WURMBRAND

preachers usually avoid doing this. They speak about the example of Christ, not their own. Is this reasonable?

A madman once asked the cook in an asylum, "Are you able to prepare good food that makes those who eat it look fit and healthy?"

The cook answered, "I surely do."

The madman said, "You'd better become a mental patient in our institution, because you are the cook yet you yourself are thin and pale."

How can someone show me the right doctrine, the right manner of living, the right faith and the right charity, if he does not have them himself? Example is the best witness and the best sermon.

If the apostle gave himself as an example to be followed, it does not mean that he had a sinless life. Only One is sinless. But Christ "was delivered [to death] for our offences, and was raised again for our justification" (Romans 4:25). So I am justified, that is, "I'm just-as-if-I'd never sinned." And I can give myself as a model to be followed by others as I myself strive to become more and more Christlike.

Twenty years ago an Italian magazine told of a Catholic priest, Alexander Zavatta, who had spent ten years in a Soviet prison camp. He asserted at that time that there were still millions of innocents in Soviet jails, and he described the tortures to which he had been subjected in order to force him to make accusations against other Christians. Fearing that he might crack because of the great pain, he stretched out his tongue and bit it as hard as he could, hoping in his despair to cut it off so as not to become a traitor. Fortunately he did not succeed. Since the council of Nicea in 325 A.D., self-mutilation has been considered unlawful for a Christian. The priest knew it, but he tried something unlawful in order to remain loyal to his Christian brethren.

Another Christian prisoner in Cuba was asked to sign a statement containing charges against brethren that would lead to their arrest. He said, "The chain keeps me from signing this."

The Communist officer protested, "But you are not in chains."

"I am," said the Christian. "I am bound by the chain of witnesses who throughout the centuries gave their lives for Christ. I am a link in this chain. I will not break it."

Thomas Aquinas, after calling martyrdom the greatest proof of perfect love, adds: "Words pronounced by martyrs before the authorities are not human words, the simple expression of a human conviction, but words pronounced by the Holy Spirit through the confessors of faith."

We too are links in this chain. We can learn from the martyrs.

~37~

FEEDING ON
BEAUTIFUL EXAMPLES

HE APOSTLE PAUL WROTE, "PUT ON THE NEW MAN, which after God is created in righteousness and true holiness" (Ephesians 3:24).

Ordinarily, men confuse holiness with goodness, though they are very different virtues. "God saw every thing that He had made, and, behold, it was very good" (Genesis 1:31). After this "very good" followed something entirely different: "God blessed the seventh day and sanctified it" (Genesis 2:3). Sanctification belongs to another sphere than goodness. A man can be very good without being holy, set apart for God. There are extreme cases when men are holy without being good. Where is the goodness of Gideon, Jael, Joshua? They were fighters for the triumph of the chosen people. In this they were holy. Whoever reads the lives of Athanasius, Luther, or Calvin sees very little trace of goodness in them. They fought ruthlessly for a truth entrusted to them, relentlessly confronting their adversaries. The truth must be victorious.

We have this commandment: to become holy by putting on the new man. But how can someone "put on a new man" in reality? The answer is, by feeding upon the right spiritual food.

Worms that live in darkness have been conditioned to prefer the light. As often as they withdrew into darkness, they would get electric shocks, whereas if they came out into the light they would find abundant food. In time, these creatures "put on a new worm." Contrary to the habit of their species, they preferred light to darkness. Then these worms were cut up into small pieces and added to the food given to other worms, and marvel of marvels, these worms also changed their habits. The RNA in their cells, the depository of memory, had programmed them differently. Similar experiments have been performed on other animals.

If you desire to put on the new man, a man of righteousness and holiness, feed upon Christ, who called himself the bread of life. He became flesh in order that He might become your daily food. Feed also on the example of saints and martyrs.

By beholding we become changed. A person who feeds his mind on the levity of television shows, who reads bad books or chooses evil company, becomes superficial in his attitudes and evil in his behavior. But by faith you can put on the new man without any effort, by beholding Jesus and by letting your spirit feed on the beautiful examples of faith given by the martyrs. This is why I write about so many.

At one time I was in prison with the Adventist pastor Boian of Ploiesti. Released on the same day as I, he was asked by a Communist officer, "What will you do now?"

He answered, "I will begin again my Christian work, with or without your permission, exactly where I left off when you arrested me."

He kept his word. Eventually he appeared before court again. The judge asked him, "Do you believe that Jesus will return and destroy His enemies?"

"He surely will."

"Will He destroy me also?"

"Without the slightest doubt I can assure you that you will be destroyed exactly like the others if you don't repent."

The judge went on, "Do you regret having preached illegally?"

"Why do you have stupid laws that forbid what is pleasing to the Lord? If you apply them, God will punish you here and in eternity."

"You were not allowed by us to preach." (In Communist countries, pastors must be licensed by the government.)

Boian's answer was, "God not only allowed me to preach, but commanded me to do so. Read the order yourself in the Bible. You will find it in Matthew 28:19-20."

He was sentenced to eight years in prison. He already had three years of jail behind him.

Such fearlessness is an excellent food for souls. By looking at these examples of courage, by looking upon Christ who has inspired them, we put on, without effort, the new man, just as worms put on "the new worm." A new breed of Christians appears, shunning comfort and seeking new spheres of zealous activity.

38

SUFFERING NOT AN
UNCONQUERABLE OBSTACLE

ISHOP VLADIMIR GHICA DIED FOR CHRIST IN the Jilava jail of Romania (where I, too, was once imprisoned). When ordained, he had prayed, "Lord, take my heart and never give it back to me. Why was I born if not to love you passionately?" His last words on his deathbed were these: "May the pains inflicted upon me, united to your pain, O Lord, heal and bless those who tortured me to death." Too often when we are wronged by others we become resentful and bitter, instead of putting our sufferings in the service of those who inflict them. Let us learn from saints like this bishop to shed every tear and to utter every groan in the spirit of self-sacrificing love for those who wrong us. Enlarge your bosom by making all these lives yours.

Jail is no hindrance to a useful Christian life.

The American bishop Walsh, who spent twenty years in a solitary prison cell in China, wrote: "I woke up one morning and found myself in jail. The word of the Lord came to me: 'This is what you dreamed of—time to say all the prayers you want to.' I could not pray much while I was working. But now I had time to pray for my family, for friends, for everyone under the sun. Prayer is powerful."

If you are depressed, forsaken, idled, bereaved, do as Bishop Walsh did. When I have bouts of depression and am no good for any work, I pray in a depressed manner until the depression is gone. Jesus himself "offered up prayers and supplications with vehement cries and tears" (Hebrews 4:7). At the end of such prayers He could say to others, "I leave you my joy."

Liu Xiaobo was a leader of the protest on Tiananmen Square in Beijing, China, which ended in a massacre. He himself was arrested. But in jail he stopped thinking only about the sins of the Communist oppressors, when the word of the Lord came to him through a Christian fellow prisoner. Realizing his own sinfulness, he wrote, "How can a person who has no sense of sin ever hear the voice of God?" He thought to himself, "Jesus was nailed to the Cross because of His love for sinners. But Christians I have known in China and those in the West don't come forward to sacrifice themselves for the sins of others. For many, religion has become another form of entertainment."

He changed his perspective: "Instead of fighting Communists because they do sinful things, I must dedicate myself to them, even unto death. If not, we all remain at the bottom of the same chasm instead of climbing to the peaks above. If anti-Communists don't love the Communists ardently and become willing to die for them, instead of fighting against them, it is like a paraplegic fighting a quadriplegic."

His thoughts may be useful to us in our conflicts with others. They can help us ascend to the peaks.

-39-

ENLARGE YOUR SELF

*P*LEASE READ ATTENTIVELY, BECAUSE I WOULD like to offer you something that will appeal to your self-interest and still satisfy your most basic spiritual needs and drives.

You and I are by nature insignificant. We dislike some of the shallowness of our work and amusements. All our thoughts are much too petty. The self, however, can be enlarged. I will tell you how.

A friend has been described by Plato as one soul in two bosoms. Friendship makes one live the beauty of two lives at once. The Church of Christ has been created by God as a fellowship of friends. It is written that after the descent of the Holy Spirit at Pentecost "the multitude of them that believed were of one heart and of one soul" (Acts 4:32). How huge this heart and this soul were! Between Jonathan and David in the Old Testament was a friendship like that. "Jonathan was knit with the soul of David and Jonathan loved him as his own soul" (1 Samuel 18:1). He did not hesitate a moment in renouncing even the throne to the benefit of his friend.

This is one of the great benefits the real Church of Christ has to offer—a tremendous opportunity for growth and enrichment with the experience of saints all over the world. You can share in the most beautiful Christian lives.

The Russian psychiatrist Dr. Nikolai Rozanov was an ascetic who never had money except what he needed for charity. Because he told his patients, "Trust in God," he was sentenced to five years of prison. He had engaged in forbidden religious propaganda by saying these few words.

Eventually he left prison strengthened in his faith, and always greeted people with the old Russian Christian greeting, "May God save you." He continued to go to church and even sang in the choir. For this he was placed for an additional four years in a psychiatric asylum. As a result of the injections he received there, he could no longer control his arms and legs. Before regaining his freedom, he paid in death the ultimate price for his faith.

The Soviet Underground Church produced many men like this who were steadfast in the faith amid sufferings. We have the privilege of enlarging our own self by becoming one in heart and soul with such individuals. They, in turn, are one in heart and soul with Christ. Union with such saints is also union with God.

~40~

COURAGEOUS NUNS

A DOCUMENT SPREAD SECRETLY IN THE SOVIET Union tells the story of a large group of nuns in a labor camp who had refused to work for the antichrist. They had been manacled and reduced to hunger. All was to no avail. Common prisoners were converted under their influence. They now had a real convent in the camp. When Irene, the daughter of the prison camp's director, fell gravely sick, he had no choice. He asked for the nuns' prayers. The girl was healed.

The wife of the Communist officer Tcherednitchenko had a difficult birth. Her life and the life of the child were in danger. One of the nuns suggested to him, "Promise the nurse that if everything goes well, you will baptize the child."

"I can lose everything by this."

"Well, choose between what you call 'everything' on one hand and your wife and child on the other."

The birth went well, and he baptized the child. He lost his job. The new commander wanted to compel the nuns to abandon their religious vestments and to wear the uniform of prisoners. They answered, "We will not wear the badge of the antichrist." They were compelled to walk naked through the snow at a freezing temperature. They went, singing the "Our Father." Not one of them fell sick. When a Communist asked the camp's atheist doctor, a Mrs. Bravermann, how this was medically possible, she replied, "Didn't you hear them singing about a Father in heaven? Well, this is the scientific explanation."

Our mission has taken up the defense of these persecuted Christians. We could help martyrs with a piece of bread, but they shared with us their nameless joy, their being true to the Truth, Christ the Lord.

~41~

CONSIDERED FOOLS

*I*N FORCED LABOR CAMPS THE WORK QUOTAS WERE high. The hungry prisoners could not fulfill them, so they were punished by being given less food. Amid sufferings like these, the Christians of Frunze (USSR) could write, "We pray for our persecutors, that the Lord may give them repentance. We ask the children of God to pray with us for a spiritual awakening of our nation." They might have had to walk through a snowstorm to their slave labor camp. But they lived separated from the much worse storms of hate and doubt. They loved and believed, they looked upon men as friends and embraced them all in their heart. Their life was rich. Their sacrifice still burns bright. We are all called to this high stage of salvation.

In a Lithuanian court the priest Seskevicius showed much courage. The prosecutor had asked that he be punished because he taught religion, which is opposed to science. Seskivicius answered, "If religion hinders the progress of science, may I put the question: Who were the first to set foot on the moon? The believers or the unbelievers? They were believers." The first food eaten on the moon was holy communion (by an American astronaut who has since become an evangelist). Seskevicius also said to his judges, "To answer violence with violence is not difficult. It is the natural reaction of all beings. But not to react is a sign of superior spiritual force." He did not react. He went quietly to prison. Others did react. Christians fought the Soviet troops on the streets of Kaunas in defense of their imprisoned priests.

A. Jaugelis was sentenced to two years for having printed secretly The Chronicle of the Catholic Lithuanian Church. How happy he must be in his prison cell, that God gave him the grace to say as his last words before court: "Millions of martyrs suffered and died for Christ and the truth preached by Him. You atheists should not have the illusion that there are no more such heroes who have no fear to suffer for the truth, for the faith, for the church."

Christians are able to retain love for their torturers even in the worst of circumstances. The peak of Communist horrors was attained in the Romanian prison of Piteshti.

Several would sit on the belly of a prisoner to make him excrete. Then he would be forced to eat his own excrement and drink his urine. Such was the daily routine in this infamous prison. There the Christian Sherban George committed suicide. His last words were: "The Communists' crimes are too horrible. I cannot pray to God for them from a distance. I must go to Him to speak on their behalf. Do not avenge my death."

It is understood, of course, that Pastor Wurmbrand does not condone suicide. Nevertheless, the circumstances of Christians in nations where believers in Christ are persecuted, horribly tortured, and often killed for their faith can be incomprehensible for Christians in free countries, and so their actions should not be judged by us. Only Christ is capable of that.]

The Ukrainian Christians Shevtchenko, Timtshak, Solovieva, Alekseeva, Borushko, Zaborskii, and Krivoi stood trial before the court in Odessa. Brother Krivoi had already spent ten years in prison for his faith. When the court convened and the accused were asked to stand, they fell to their knees instead and one of them began to pray aloud. Why should they pay their respects to the representatives of a state that is not an authority ordained by God, but the apocalyptic beast drunk with the blood of saints? The president of the court asked our sister Alekseeva why she refused to have an attorney. Her reply was, "I have long since taken Jesus Christ as my defender. My witness is in heaven and my record is on high" (Job 16:19). Shevtchenko also refused to have an attorney, saying, "An atheist cannot defend a believer. God is my protector."

Hundreds of Christians had gathered outside the court-house. Because they were not allowed to enter, they waited outside during the long bitterly cold hours. The accused refused to answer a single question until their brethren were allowed to enter. And they won—many came in to watch!

So the Baptists in chains decided who would enter the court-room, not the Communist authorities. Never comply, always resist. This is the lesson which we can take from these heroes of faith. Resist, fight, and you will succeed.

The transcript of this trial tells us the most appalling things. We will mention only one. The Communists charged that the Russian Baptists had cut the veins of the one to be baptized and then all the believers had drunk of his blood.

Not since Nero's time have such mad lies been told about Christians. Sister Solovieva was accused, among other charges, of organizing a group of young Christians to help an elderly lady work her garden. She said in her own defense, "Article 176 of the law of cults forbids churches to give material assistance to their members. [To help someone work his garden is therefore a punishable act, if it is done by a church member.] I wish to tell the court that to my knowledge nowhere, not even in the most retrograde country, can the law ask the right to control how I use money honestly earned and forbid that I should give it to those in need."

Then Sister Solovieva became the accuser of the Soviets before world opinion, as she said to them, "The legislation about cults has as its aim to deprive the believers of the most elementary rights of citizens. It commits genocide. The existing legislation puts us in such a position as to make the existence of believers impossible . . . I don't consider the spreading of

Christian literature a crime. I spread literature and will continue to do so whenever I have the slightest opportunity."

She went to prison for this.

(What about those of us who are free to spread Christian literature? When did you last give out a Christian publication? If you are interested in doing so, contact us. Our mission can supply very effective Christian literature for free distribution.)

Brother Timtshak began his defense with these words: "I consider myself happy to sit on the bench of the accused not as a thief or a murderer or someone who meddles in another's business. I rejoice about my situation which I am in for Christ's sake . . . In my sermons I preached about the love of God. I told how Christ loved men even unto death on the Cross, so that everyone who believes in Him might have life everlasting. I have preached this, I preach it today, and I will continue to preach it."

Brother Krivoi said in his final words, "Suffering as a Christian, I am ready to wear chains. I have been a believer for forty years (ten of which were spent in Siberian prisons). You will not re-educate me and you will not break me with threats."

These brothers and sisters of ours were sentenced to Siberia, to the land of the white death. There they performed slave labor in ragged clothing. They stood kneedeep in swamps and in snow. Their food was meager and the physically weak among them died. But their names will remain forever written in heaven and in the hearts of Christians everywhere.

The pastors of the official Russian church, who willingly inform on their own flock, considered these martyrs fools. Even some American Christian magazines declared the attitude of these martyrs "unwise." The accusation is not new. Peter considered it unwise for Jesus to go to His death. Brethren begged Paul not to go to Jerusalem. The name of St. Paul remains. Who today remembers his kind advisers or critics?

Charles Spurgeon, the celebrated Baptist preacher, once said, "I cannot do otherwise than contend with those who contend with God." These Russian martyrs belong in the same category as he.

~42~

SUFFERING FOR
ANOTHER'S CRIME

A PRIEST BY THE NAME OF NIKIFOROV-
Volghin tells in his book *Dust on the Road*
about an encounter he had in prison with a
Christian, who told him this story:

> *Once I came home and heard a cry. I found my wife
> dead, stabbed in the heart by an acquaintance. The
> murderer fell at my feet asking forgiveness. I said to
> him, "Go, and never do this again." Then I went to
> the police and took responsibility for the crime. I was
> given a sentence.*
>
> *In Krasnoiarsk jail, one prisoner killed another. I
> took this crime upon myself, also. I am sentenced for
> life. I could not do otherwise. Loving God, I look
> upon all men as upon angels. My only prayer is, "I am
> yours and you are mine. Have mercy on me." I would
> not have told you these things had you not been a
> priest. You asked me why I am here, and I owed you
> the truth.*

I was present when this prisoner died. It was as if heaven had opened. The prisoner's last words were, "Lord, I would like to continue to suffer for others, but thy will be done."

What a high calling—to suffer for what others had done! This means, to imitate Jesus exactly.

Once we received an eyewitness report about the stoning to death of a Christian girl in a Communist labor camp. She was bound hand and foot and made to kneel in the center of a circle of people, who were commanded to stone her. Those who refused to do so were shot. She died with her face shining like St. Stephen. One at least of those who saw her then was led to faith in Christ through that girl who sealed her testimony with her blood.

A young man prayed for his persecutors as he hung six days on a cross before he died. Five students who were sent out to dig deep holes, in which they were put alive, sang Christian hymns as they were buried.

The Chinese abbot Tong, decapitated by the Reds for his faith, said, "Toward the Communist initiatives, only one attitude is possible. It is to say 'no' and to give your head. If we start a dialogue with them where Communism has power, we are lost." Another Chinese martyr, Pastor Tsand, gave this advice: "If you are arrested, your conduct can be only this: silence."

Brother Kozlov, a man who spent ten years in prison for robbery, was converted in jail and afterwards spent ten years in prison for Christ in the Soviet Union. Risking a new arrest, he wrote to "Kosygin, Brezhnev & Co., Butchers, Inc.": "If you would not prevent Christians who are in prisons even today from speaking about Christ to this miserable world, how much the life of thousands of sinners would be changed! You would not need to keep one million atheist lecturers propagating an atheist morale."

Courage and continual unrelenting attacks succeed. Kozlov was actually called to a hearing by Soviet rulers. The converted robber spoke to the impenitent robbers as on Golgotha. The one who stole a couple of hundred rubles witnessed for Christ to those who have stolen one-third of the world. But God can do miracles. There are strong indications that Brezhnev died as a convert.

The heroism of Christian martyrs spreads its perfume in spite of the horrors. In one case, male guards tore the clothes off of nuns and carried them naked through the prison yard. The prison walls are thick. Their cries of shame do not reach the free world, where most Christians sleep undisturbed. A group of thirty Orthodox Christians refused to wear the badge showing their number as prisoners. They were children of God. A child of God does not allow himself to be reduced to a number. Each one is a jewel apart. They declared quietly, "We will not work for Satan and we will not lift our hats before you Communist officers. We show reverence only to God." For this they were punished with half a year in solitary confinement, in unheated small cells where there was scarcely room to turn around. Food was given only every third day. The group passed before the prison director. Approaching him, everyone signed himself with the sign of the cross and exorcized him with the words, "Perish, Satan."

43

RUSSIAN BELIEVERS IN PSYCHIATRIC ASYLUMS

WHILE MANY OF OUR BRETHREN WERE IN prison, some were in psychiatric asylums. There, too, they praised God. Brother Shimanov wrote from an asylum:

The bedlam, the anxiety about my family, the tension of my nerves all destroy me. But if they drive me mad or if I remain sane, I accept everything God sends, as a child accepts everything from the hand of his father: the sweet and the bitter, folly or reason, light or darkness, every disaster and all clarity. Cowardice is unreasonable. In the asylum, I have thought often that the will of God keeps intact the freedom of man.

We too should lay aside our grumbling and complaining and accept with good grace all the things that befall us. Jesus accepted flogging, mockery, death on the Cross, an early tomb, and the descent into hell. A glorious resurrection followed for Him. It will follow for us too, if in all circumstances—even in maddening ones we keep saying, "Let God be magnified."

Where did these Christians get such strength? From a source available to all of us: prayer. Perhaps we can learn from them.

Natalia Gorbanevskaya, who was put in the section for the mentally ill in the Butyrka prison in Moscow, composed the following prayer, which she repeated again and again.

Don't crush me, Lord, don't lose me like a card in a lost game. Don't reject me so as to make me wander through the world not believing anything. You walked on the sea as if it had been dry land. No obstacle can hinder your steps. Don't send me out into this world of suffering without a firm staff, without aim and support. You, God and Son of Man, if it was Your will to put on these shoulders the yoke which makes chains rattle at every step; don't allow my soul to freeze outside in the ice, in the cold night.

The Soviet Hebrew Christian Krasnov-Levitin described his time in jail.

When I was in prison, I lived every day in the spirit of the liturgy. At eight in the morning I began to walk to and fro in my cell and said the words of the liturgy. In doing so, I felt united with Christendom in the whole world . . . The prison walls pulled back. The whole universe, the visible and the invisible, became my habitation . . . After the liturgy I felt a spiritual elation, clarity and inner purity.

Such prayers work. Levitin says that "there is no power in the world that can resist the power of God" obtained by prayer.

This assertion must, however, be qualified. The godly character of a newborn person cannot be broken, but the organ through which it expresses itself is the brain—oneand-a-half pounds of tissue, subject to all the laws of matter. Communists destroyed the brains of some believers through doping, hunger, sleep deprivation, and beating on the head. Some Christians treated in this manner beyond endurance could no longer resist.

The most tragic example I know is that of Nikolai Moiseev. He was exposed to the worst treatment for eight years in an asylum, in which he was interned because of his faith. When in the end his family was allowed to visit him, he did not recognize them. They spoke about Jesus. There was no response. He no longer recognized the name. He had sacrificed for Christ more than anyone else: his faith in Christ. Neither the once-cherished name nor the word Christ meant anything to him.

I am sure this man is saved. I would like to have a place like his in heaven. The Communists were able to destroy the most precious organ of his outward man, but like all of us he had the hidden man of the heart, which the poison chemicals did not reach. This hidden man was in the embrace of Christ during those torturous years.

We were spared the worst. We can at least pray and thus obtain strength.

In Psalm 138:1, we read, "I will praise thee with my whole heart." The highest form of praise I know is to become silent, overawed by the majesty of God. Kneel silently in adoration before the One who shows His glory in His saints. Here words cease.

~44~

THOSE WHO
CANNOT BE SHAKEN

HILE WE CHRISTIANS REMAIN SILENT, LET US allow our Jewish friend Shifrin to say what he saw and rejoice.

The Christians whom I met in prison were quiet and concentrated. They strongly believed that the Creator leads them the right way, and they received sufferings as blessings. They did not resist the guards in worldly things, but stood firm when their religious convictions were touched. There they could not be shaken. When I looked toward them, I sometimes felt that holy rays came from their barracks filled with holiness and prayers.

The following is a resume of an article that appeared in a Soviet newspaper (Znamia lunosti):

An old man of small size enters the dock of the court-room. He puts his hands on his breast and says, "Peace be with you, brethren and sisters. "He is a pastor. We have before us a fisher of men, who by teaching about life after death brought many victims into his clever nets. Outwardly he is a quiet missionary. From the first minute of the trial he ornaments himself with the aureole of a martyr, ready to suffer for the faith, for Christ.

In 1948 he had already been sentenced to jail once for propagation of religion. But he did not learn the lesson. He started his underground work again. What is the charge against Artem Hivuk? The following are the words of the attorney of the district of Brest Tarasenko: "For a long time, he was leader of the unregistered congregation of the 'rebellious sectarians' [the name given by the Communists to the Underground Christians]. *He propagated religion. He trespassed against the law regarding religious cults." Hivuk was extremely zealous to win the youth. And he succeeded often.*

Hivuk said to the judges, "All are equal before God. An enemy is also a friend. You have no right to hit him."

Children he won for Christ refused to join the Pioneers [a Communist children's organization] *All, beginning with the director of the school and finishing with the leader of the Pioneers, seem to have sympathized with Hivuk. They gave him liberty to work, contrary to the instructions of the Secret Police. Things went so far in the complicity of the local Soviet leaders with Hivuk that he got to the point of asking permission to use the school building for religious services. This could not be allowed, so the Christians gathered in private homes and, during the summer, in nature. There children sang "heavenly melodies."* [How heavenly these melodies must have been for Communists to call them so!] *Hivuk traveled from place to place preaching, including Moscow.*

For these "crimes" he was sentenced to many years in prison. In the free world we would not be sentenced for shedding light around us. The irony is that we so seldom avail ourselves of our opportunities.

45

THE CHOICE TO BE A SAINT

HERE STILL ARE UNNUMBERED CHRISTIAN PRISONERS throughout the world, in such places as China, Vietnam, Myanmar, and Muslim countries. What happens to them spiritually?

It would seem that the long stretches of barbed-wire fence, the watchtowers, searchlights, long columns of ragged human figures gray in the grayness of the dawn, the shouts and whistles of command that are encountered from the moment one enters prison, all depress and suffocate a person spiritually.

Valentina Saveleva wrote after her release,

> We were often knee-deep in the mud. Our coats and boots were never dry. There was no washroom. The water was not drinkable because of the salt. Many had to sleep on the dirt floor. There were not enough blankets to keep warm. When we awakened in the morning, we had to be careful not to rise too quickly, for our hair was frozen to the dirt floor It was impossible to remain free from lice. Many died of tuberculosis. Food was scarce and hardly edible. The temperature was seldom above 41 degrees Fahrenheit. The

prison was full of demon possessed criminals, who cursed day and night. They wanted to destroy my faith.

Can love be the absolute law under such circumstances, or do they justify becoming lawless? The renowned psychologist Sigmund Freud, wishing to belittle morality, asserted: "Let one attempt to expose a number of the most diverse people uniformly to hunger! With the increase of hunger, all individual differences will blur and in their stead will appear the uniform expression of the one instilled urge."

Freud had not known hunger. I have, for fourteen years in Communist jails. Hunger, like any other pain, does not produce uniform results. Under pressure, some individuals become swine and others saints. Some grabbed the little piece of bread belonging to a fellow prisoner; others renounced their only bit of bread and medicine to save another's life.

Christians know how to forgo even life itself. In Zimbabwe, a guerilla lifted his axe to kill a priest. Nearby was another priest, Killian Knoerl, who could have escaped. Instead, he chose to fight for his brother against the guerilla. He himself was killed.

The lawless have no scruples; they steal and betray, so they certainly should have. But they are neurotic and need Jesus' cure. The spiritually healthy, on the other hand, remain loving even if it means suffering pain and even death. The lawless find an excuse for their sins: fate, heredity, or environment. But though God in His providence may have allowed me to pass through trials and tribulations, how I react to them is up to me. As a free moral agent, I can choose to be guided in all things by love or I can choose to be lawless. I can be alive in Christ, certain of a future life or I can be emotionally dead on this earth.

Paul wrote four of his epistles while in jail. They contain many prayers, but not one for his release. I have read hundreds of letters from Christian prisoners, but not once do they demand prayers for their freedom. During my fourteen years in Communist prisons I composed around 350 poems, some of which were published in *Sermons in Solitary Confinement, If*

Prison Walls Could Speak and *Alone with God*. Not one shows a desire to be rid of my chains. The Romanian Christian poets Traian Dorz and Moldovanu were also in jail for many years. The songs they composed were all full of the joy produced by the suffering for a glorious cause.

In the USSR, the Communists made a film about the Lithuanian priest Svarinskas, who was in jail. The purpose of the film was to show how dangerous he was to society. Svarinskas is shown preaching: "If a priest under atheism boasts of serving a parish for twenty-five years without being driven out by the atheists, he is a bad priest. Were he good, they would have chased him out long since. Persecution is the sign that a priest fulfills his duty. Where atheism reigns, the only right place for a priest to die is in jail." The apostle Paul must have thought like this. Therefore he never prayed for his release.

The majority of our prayers are usually for release from difficult situations. But why should I pray to be released from an unhappy marriage, from the brutality of a parent, from a child who breaks my heart, or from other miseries? Missionaries have gone joyfully to savages to show them the love of Christ. Some, like John Williams and Bishop Hannington, were eaten by cannibals. They went to death reciting Jesus' words, "Love your enemies, do good to those who hate you."

We too should be patient, though the brain reels. His grace is sufficient to quell the grief.

Our brothers and sisters in jail volunteer to take beatings for others. In Auschwitz, under Hitler, Mary Skobtseva and Maximilian Kolbe stepped forward and asked to be executed in place of others. They died a martyr's death. When it was cold, prisoners gave away sweaters so that others might feel warm. I have witnessed such scenes myself.

Concern for others drowns out your own troubles. Focus on God as the saints in prison do and you will know that heavenly peace comes from patient cross-bearing. To get out of the neurosis of lawlessness, begin to practice the law of love, at least in little things. Deny yourself for a period the food you love most, or some luxury, in clothing, and think of those who eat ble food and are in rags. Interrupt your sleep for prayer lf of those interrogated during the night. Give up some cosmetics for those who cannot even wash. Renounce an hour of television for those who for years have been in solitary confinement in underground cells and see nothing. Try to be silent for a day in order to empathize with the solitary, who cannot speak to anyone for years.

Sacrifice your complaining and grumbling for one day. Take time from other preoccupations to pray for the persecuted.

RICHARD WURMBRAND

~46~

THE DUTY TO REMAIN SANE

*S*UFFERERS LEARNED UNDER TORTURE TO SEE THE horrors of prison life as no more than the buzzing of tiresome flies, because jail was like Golgotha, where there were not only crosses but also a beautiful garden (John 19:41).

Young believers learned from those matured through decades of pain. They had the best theological training, where religion is not simply taught but practiced at the highest level. Perhaps we too should look to experienced saints and sit at their feet, as our persecuted brethren have done. They lived under conditions calculated to drive one insane, with criminals and madmen whose behavior and speech were outrageously obscene. Frequently our hungry brothers and sisters were bullied with unimaginable cruelty. The syncopated beating of hundreds of agonized hearts oppressed the faithful during the night.

If we find ourselves provoked beyond endurance, let us remember and learn from our imprisoned holy brethren. They heed the voice of conscience, which tells them it is their duty to stay sane by being open to the life-giving Spirit of God. Every letter and personal contact with them revealed that they live in a realm of peace. They are burning flames on the altar of Christ.

They are kind to all, especially to their torturers who, knowing no kindness, need to benefit from a surplus from another source. No suffering is absurd if it generates such love for the wicked.

Our mission has been privileged to be constantly in touch with these saints. It has received and conveyed to the free world great inspiration from them. The National Institute of Mental Health (USA) claims that 62% of Americans suffer from a diagnosable mental illness. One half of all hospital beds in the USA are occupied by mental cases.

In other countries the situation is not much better. Our generation suffers from a widespread neurosis: lawlessness. The law is not embedded in our thinking. Everyone walks according to their own fancies without regard to the highest law: an all-absorbing, fervent love for God and humanity. If I do not have such love as a guide in all my actions, woe is me! I am sick and urgently need the cure that only Jesus can offer.

The Lord met and still meets much apathy, but He also meets ardent love. There are still souls who burn passionately for Him like the apostle John and Mary Magdalene did.

The Christian student Leonas Sileikis in Soviet Lithuania had to be examined before a commission of seven teachers. She was asked what she thought about atheist books. She replied, "They contain lies and slander."

A Communist delivered to her a speech against religion and then asked, "Do you renounce your faith?"

Her answer was, "I believe and will continue to do so."

The director of the school explained to her father, who was present, the danger of religion. He replied, "It is not true that religion is dangerous. The fruit of treading religion under your feet is that students do not respect the teachers anymore; they drink, smoke and are promiscuous."

The school director showed his wisdom: "Seeing that few go to church nowadays, it is important to join the majority."

The father answered, "Only corpses flow with the current. A living person can swim against it."

The director warned him, "With such ideas you will make it impossible for your daughter to continue her studies."

Her father replied, "It isn't I who hinders her, but you. What good is study if you have to renounce the highest value, a personal faith?"

The wise men brought to the holy Child gold, frankincense and myrrh. This family has fulfilled the commandment, with which I challenge you: "Present your bodies a living sacrifice, holy, acceptable unto God, which is your reasonable service" (Romans 12:1).

~47~

THE HAPPIEST DAY

WHEN NIJOLE SADUNAITE, A CATHOLIC, WAS sentenced in Soviet Lithuania she told the court:

Truth needs no defense, because it is all powerful and unconquerable. Only deceit and lies, being powerless before truth, need weapons, soldiers and prisons to prolong their infamous rule for a while. A biased government digs its own grave. I am on the right side and am ready to lose liberty for truth. I will gladly give even my life. Only those who love have the right to blame and criticize the objects of their love. Therefore I speak to you. You rejoice about your victory. Victory over what? Over morality? Over mean and debased men infected by fear?

Thanks be to God, not all men have compromised yet. We [Christians] are not many in society, but quality is on our side. Without fear of prison, we have to condemn all actions that lead to injustice and humiliation. We must distinguish what is written by men from what is commanded by God.

We owe to Caesar only what remains after having given to God what is His due. The most important thing in life is to free heart and mind from fear, because yielding to evil is the greatest sin.

This day is the happiest of my life. I was judged today for the cause of truth and love toward men. What cause could be more important? I have an enviable fate, a glorious destiny. My condemnation will be my triumph. I regret only having done so little for men. Standing today on the side of the eternal truth of Jesus Christ, I remember His fourth beatitude: "Blessed are they which do hunger and thirst after righteousness, for they shall be filled" (Matthew 5:6). There exists no greater joy than to suffer for truth and for one's fellow men.

How could I not rejoice when God Almighty has promised that light will overcome darkness and truth will overcome error and lies! May God give us the assurance that His last judgment will be favorable to all of us. I will ask this in prayer for you every day of my life. Let us love each other and we will be happy. Only the one who loves not is unhappy.

We must condemn evil, but we must love the man, even the one in error. This you can learn only at the school of Jesus Christ, who is the only truth for all, the only way and the only life. Good Jesus, your Kingdom comes into our souls.

She was sentenced to three years in prison. When, after being freed, she met the Pope in Rome, he asked her, "How was it in jail?" She replied, "Romantic."

We have our sorrows, troubles, apprehensions, even dramas. But she lifted before court the veil which she, like every other Christian, wears in everyday life and which makes us appear busy only with the things of this world, even if they are good works. She beheld with open face the glory of God and was changed into the same image of our Redeemer (2 Corinthians 3:18).

We, too, are called—we, too, can resist sinful surroundings.

Evghenii Pushkov was a Baptist music student in Russia who had advanced to the point of playing in the Philharmonic. But he knew he could further his career only by renouncing his faith, since the Soviets would not allow a witnessing Christian to affirm himself in the arts. One day, he invited his father and wife to the concert. The orchestra played Tchaikovsky's lovely "Dying Swan" based on the legend that the swan sings only once in life, just before its death. Evghenii put all his heart into the music; he had decided that it would be his own swan song. He would henceforth prefer Jesus. His family, sensing his decision, were in tears. After the concert, he embraced them and said, "Henceforth you will not weep for me any more. I dedicate myself wholly to the Lord." Sadly, such a decision in a Communist country does not banish tears. He went to prison for his faith.

In a Soviet prison there was a Lithuanian Christian lady who as a child had looked down from the attic and seen the Communists kill her whole family of eight, then leave laughing. After that she never spoke. Sentenced to 25 years, she spent them in perfect silence. Only once, in the beginning, did she tell her story to one inmate. After that, she spent all her free time walking alone to and fro through the prison yard, in sunshine, rain, and snow. She bore her burden in silence without ever grumbling. She had seen God face to face.

How do we bear our lesser tragedies?

The Orthodox bishop Andrew was sentenced to death. The story is told that before the execution, he asked to be allowed to pray. As he knelt, he simply was no more. The henchmen were in a panic, knowing they would lose their lives if he disappeared. After an hour he reappeared, on his knees in prayer, surrounded by a luminous cloud. The sentence was carried out, but one of the henchmen was converted and told the story.

If it is difficult for you to believe such a tale, then listen to this one. A child came home from Sunday school and told his mother, "We were taught that when the Jews under Joshua had to cross the Jordan, the soldiers built a pontoon bridge, while planes were hovering in the sky to protect them."

The mother objected: "Surely you could not have been taught that."

"No, mother. But if I told you that I was taught a miracle happened and the Jordan was divided so God's people went across on dry land, you would not have believed it."

I believe in biblical miracles. I believe miracles happen even today. The greatest miracle is that the henchman was converted. The fantasy of this man who passed in one minute from a readiness to kill a saint to becoming a saint himself works powerfully. It also makes him see things that might not have happened. Those who witness God's miracles become very sure of their beliefs.

-48-

PRAISE GOD IN SUFFERING

"A BISHOP MUST BE ... A LOVER OF GOOD" (Titus 1:8, according to the original).

In the first Church "bishop" was not a rank in a hierarchy. All the elders of the church were considered bishops (in Greek, *episkopos*) through the empowering of the Holy Spirit (cf Acts 20:17–28). Even our English word "elder of the church" is misleading. These elders were sometimes very young, as was the case with Timothy. The Greek word for elder means "far seeing."

In plain English, the Scripture quoted above means "an overseer of the church, a church leader, whatever his name—bishop, pastor, priest, preacher, mission director—must be "a lover of good." The highest good is to have God living in one's innermost being. A church leader must love to bring men to this stage, to teach them to deny their selves until nothing remains but God. A church leader must also do this work when persecution comes. Some 40,000 clergymen were killed by the Communists, because they fulfilled their duty. Lenin, Stalin, Khrushchev, Kosygin, Mao, Ceausescu, and other butchers were responsible for their deaths.

We thank God that the Church has self-sacrificing leaders. The Russian pastor Serghei Golev had been in prison 22 years when his wife came to visit him. She was forbidden to do so because it was discovered that he had a New Testament in hiding. She could see him only from afar, but still she could see that he was in tears. She shouted to him, "I never saw you weeping. Strengthen yourself. Soon everything will end."

From behind the barbed wire, he answered, "I got tired. Greet all those who sincerely love the Lord."

Strength returned to him when, after this, several brethren discussed in the prison cell how they would like to die. One said, "I wish to die while serving the Church. Let her bury me." Another, "I desire to be with my family, to bring my children to faith and then to die." Pastor Golev, who had that one moment of weakness, said, "I wish to die in prison. Here I passed my best years. Straight from here to the Lord—this is my prayer."

We had this communication from the Underground Church itself. Her communications contain no idle talk. She tells with soberness and humility the story of her heavy suffering, but also praises God for the endurance he has given her amid tribulations.

The same communication tells the story of Sister Nadejda Sloboda. No one would call her a pastor. But she was the first one in her village to be converted through gospel broadcasting in Russian (a work our mission engages in). Don't call her a pastor—but the fact is that she formed a church in her village. The church grew so mightily that the police had to surround the village to keep people from the collective farms around from coming to hear its message. Sister Sloboda was sentenced for this to four years of prison. Her five children were forcibly taken to an atheistic boarding school. Her husband remained alone.

In prison, Sister Sloboda was confined for two months in an unheated, isolated cell, where she had to sleep on the concrete floor without a mattress, all because she had told other prisoners about Christ. During the day she worked. Everybody wondered how she could endure it. She answered, "I fall asleep on the cold concrete floor trusting in God and it becomes warm around me. I rest in the arms of God."

RICHARD WURMBRAND

The prison director suggested to her that she make a request to be freed from this punishment. She answered, "It was not I who decided to be put in this cell. It is not for me to ask to be released from it." We are reminded of St. Paul's refusal to leave the prison in Philippi until the magistrates came and besought him to do so (Acts 16:36-39). Such stars exist in the Christian firmament.

Attending churches in the free world, I sometimes say to myself, "If the day of God's judgment were a fashion show, many in this congregation would be saved." Our imprisoned sister Sloboda is clothed in the righteousness of Christ and in the zeal to make God manifest in her life.

In China, a sword was put to the chest of a Christian, who was asked, "Are you a Christian?"

He answered, "Yes."

He would have been killed if an officer had not said, "Free him; he is an idiot."

Someone asked him later, "How could you confess Christ with such courage?"

He replied, "I had read the story of Peter's denial of Jesus, and I did not wish to weep bitterly."

It is stupid to fear those who can kill only the body, instead of fearing the one who can throw body and soul into Gehenna.

The martyr Otto Wiebe wrote before his death in a Soviet prison: "It is a great joy for me to suffer for my Savior. This is not something unexpected but has been a conscious choice from early youth. And this is proof of His divine power, which enables a child of God to bear in surrender, quietly, to His honor the cross He lays on us." He left behind eight children. Such martyr families should be helped, but we should also learn from those who give their lives for Christ. Brother Wiebe died in prison after having shared the prophetic calling of his church to oppose devilish Marxism. He died praising God. We, too, can learn to praise God in our sufferings.

49

LOVE "WITH ALL YOUR VERY MUCH"

ICAELA WAS AN ORTHODOX NUN WHO believed that the Communion bread and wine were really the body and blood of our Lord. When the Soviet Army entered the Vladimireshti convent in Romania, she defended the altar with her body. Thrown in prison, she was mistreated beyond description. But from her solitary cell she tapped out prayers in Morse code through the wall to fellowprisoners until she died.

In another Romanian prison, some guards, pretending to be sympathetic, inquired of female prisoners about their children's birthdays. Those particular days were then chosen to give them severe beatings with rubber truncheons.

Weeping was forbidden. If a mother wept after being beaten, she was beaten again.

In jail, the temptation to abandon the faith is always present. The devil whispers, "Howl with the wolves, and the suffering will end." But Christians do not wish the suffering to end at the cost of their faith. Those who proclaim that being a Christian means prosperity, health, and well-being preach "another gospel which is not a gospel" (Galatians 1:6–7). Why should

Christians desire to escape suffering when it is written about them that they take "pleasure in infirmities, in reproaches, in necessities, in persecution, in distresses for Christ's sake" (2 Corinthians 12:10)? Who wants to escape pleasure?

When I was in a Romanian Communist prison, our feet were swollen with edema caused by hunger. At times we had only one slice of bread a week. Rats jumping over our faces awoke us at night. Occasionally the wind brought a tree leaf into the barren yard in which we walked, and it reminded us that a world of trees, flowers, and joy still existed. A daisy had succeeded in growing between the stones in the yard. I plucked its petals, saying over each one, "She loves me, with joy, with sorrow, with little, or nothing." The last petal told me that my wife Sabina, who was in another jail, loved me with sorrow.

The cell walls did not tell us that story of those who had been there before us. If we were to die in this cell, the walls would still remain silent. We often felt forsaken, unremembered. The temptation to join the world of wickedness and deceit in order to go free was great. Under totally different circumstances, we all have such temptations. But by the grace of God we had made the decision, like Job, not to speak wickedly and not to utter deceit. Our words will continue to speak of love and faith and truth. God has helped many to fulfill this promise.

In prison our brothers and sisters learn Christlikeness, likeness to the Man of Sorrows.

Twenty times a night they would be awakened by the guards who watched them through the peephole. "Take your hands out from under the blanket!" "Turn your face to the door!" "Dress yourself for interrogation!" Their eyes would be blindfolded, and like the blind they would be taken before torturers and would not know from which side the next blow would come.

Prisoners were hungry. But a more formidable problem even than eating was going to the toilet. This was a favor granted by the Communists only after pleadings that sometimes lasted a whole night. Even then, female prisoners often had to fulfill their needs in the presence of males.

Our brethren in the faith endured all this, remaining good and faithful. No bad or wicked word escaped their lips. We should emulate their example in our trials and resolve to guard the words of our mouth and the meditation of our heart, that they may be acceptable in the eyes of Him who loves us and gave His life for our sins.

Brother Michael Ershov spent forty-three years in Soviet jails for his faith in Christ. Time and distance quench small loves, but increase great ones. During those years his love for Christ burned ever more brightly as He walked the way of the cross. Such faith seems overdrawn. Everything exaggerated becomes insignificant. But there exists no possibility of exaggeration in the mutual love between God and man. On both sides it is a love with all one's heart, with all one's soul, with all one's might (Deuteronomy 6:5). In the Hebrew original it is not "with all thy might," but *bekol meodha,* which means literally "with all your very much."

PART 8

CHILDREN OF THE FAITHFUL

~*50*~

SACRIFICING THE DEAREST

GIRL NAMED MARY TELLS THE STORY OF THE court trial in Russia in which her mother was deprived of parental rights. The Communists shouted at her, "You are a mother. Deny God. What did he give you? Whom do you love more, your own children or your idol? How can you?"

Her mother sat with her scarf covering her eyes, repeating, "God sees everything. He will reward."

When Mary and the other children cried to her, "Mother, do not leave us!" she did not even turn to them.

It is a scene exactly like those we read about in the history of the early martyrs, who went into the circus arena to be devoured by wild beasts and would not listen to the pleading of their loved ones who asked them to recant and save their lives, for their children's sake. With God, it was the mystery of preferring the death of His Son to permitting the eternal death of sinners. With saints, it is the mystery of preferring to lose their children rather than to deny God. Such is our God—so are we. We can do nothing but sing His praises, whatever the consequences. The story of Mary shows the strength of a mother's faith. Now let's look at the example of a child. Many little ones often excel in Christian virtues.

A missionary couple named Barendsen—he Dutch, she Finnish—went to Afghanistan to preach the gospel, knowing they would encounter both Communist and Muslim terrorism. Being one in spirit with Christ, they were ready to give their lives for Him. Both were stabbed to death. At their burial, their five-year-old son said loudly, "I am a Christian. I forgive the murderers of my parents." We know of one Muslim who was converted after hearing this child, who had an intimate knowledge of Jesus.

In Almanach St. Peter Clavier 1990, Amelio Crotti, who had been a prisoner in China, wrote:

> *From my cell I heard a mother speak soothing words to her child of five. She had been arrested with the child because she had protested against the arrest of her bishop. All the prisoners were indignant at seeing the suffering of the child. Even the prison director said to the mother, "Don't you have pity on your daughter? It is sufficient for you to declare that you give up being a Christian and will not go to church any more. Then you and the child will be free. "*
>
> *In despair, the woman agreed and was released.*
>
> *After two weeks she was forced to shout from a stage before 10,000 people, "I am no longer a Christian."*
>
> *On their return home, the child, who had stood near her when she denied her faith, said, "Mummy, today Jesus is not satisfied with you. "*
>
> *The mother explained, "You wept in prison. I had to say this out of love for you."*
>
> *Siao-Mei replied, "I promise that if we go to jail again for Jesus, I will not weep."*
>
> *The mother ran to the prison director and told him, "You convinced me I should say wrong things for my daughter's sake, but she has more courage than I."*
>
> *Both went back to prison. But Siao-Mei no longer wept.*

Jesus was born in a stable. Children of Christians have been in dreary, damp prison cells with heroic mothers who remind us in their saintliness of the holy virgin Mary.

A Russian, Vladimir Tatishtshev, was arrested in Shanghai. The authorities had iron tubes put on his legs, which they then tightened with screws and hammered until they broke his bones, to make him confess imaginary crimes. He refused. Then the Communist police went to his home. An officer picked up Tatishtshev's baby and told the mother, "If you don't sign an accusation against the prisoner, we will smash your child's head." The mother could not believe that such a thing could happen, so she refused. Then the police officer, a woman herself, smashed the head of the baby against the wall. The mother stabbed the officer, and the other Communists shot the mother.

Three corpses! Sin unto death. Countless episodes of this nature took place, and still happen in Red China, not to mention India, Tibet, Sudan, and North Vietnam. The free world knows little of real suffering.

The Communist newspaper Uchitelskaia Gazeta revealed that in the village of Burnii a teacher wrote on the blackboard, "There is no God" and asked the children to read it. One girl raised her hand, stood up, and read loudly and clearly, "God exists." The children told the teacher the Parable of the Prodigal Son. The teacher, Matrena Matveeva, complained that all her pupils were children of believers. Every pupil in the village! She organized an atheist festival. Not even one child came. The children spent two to three hours a day in prayer. You might say that is too much for children. How many hours do American children spend watching television?

When we read in the Bible that blessings are promised to children of the faithful, some of us expect a good material position, a happy marriage, high degrees, and positions of honor. But the Bible never deceives us about what is understood by "blessings." The Lord Jesus said, "Blessed are they which are persecuted for righteousness' sake: for theirs is the kingdom of heaven. Blessed are ye, when men shall revile you, and persecute you, and shall say all manner of evil against you falsely, for my sake" (Matthew 5: 10-11).

Christians know only one sadness—not to be saints. They have one suffering—not to share enough the sufferings of Christ and their fellow men. When sorrows are given to their children because they have the right attitude in life, Christians rejoice and count them as blessings. I write these things as a parent, grandparent, and great-grandparent myself, having searched my heart thoroughly to determine what I wish for my children and grandchildren. I desire for them "the fellowship of Christ's sufferings," that "they might be made conformable unto His death" so "that they might attain to the resurrection from the dead" (Philippians 3:10–11).

RICHARD WURMBRAND

-51-

SPECIAL CHILDREN

"It shall come to pass, if thou shalt hearken diligently unto the voice of the Lord thy God, to observe and to do all His commandments which I command thee this day . . . blessed shall be the fruit of thy body" (Deuteronomy 28:1, 4).

I THOUGHT ABOUT THIS PROMISE OF GOD WHEN I read the second volume of Solzhenitsyn's *The Gulag Archipelago*. A Christian writer and Nobel prize winner, he was expelled from Russia by the Soviet government. He relates the story of a Russian couple named Leshtshev, who had been imprisoned for their faith. They left children behind who grew up richly blessed, because their parents hearkened to the voice of God even when it meant heavy suffering. The children also had the privilege of being imprisoned for their belief in Christ. This was their blessing, which once more was multiplied. They too had children, all of whom were sent to concentration camps for their adherence to Christ.

All, that is, except Zoia, who was ten years old. She was put in a home for children to be re-educated. There she declared that she would never part with the cross her mother put around her neck just before leaving the house in handcuffs. To be very sure that the Reds would not take the cross away from her while she slept, she bound the chain tightly around her neck. Considered incurable, Zoia was sent to a home for mentally deficient children. Here she continued the fight for her cross and for the Savior whom it symbolized. When other children tried to teach her to blaspheme and steal, she answered, "A holy woman like my mother should not have a criminal child."

She brought several of her schoolmates to faith. As in any school at that time, there was a statue of Stalin in the yard. These children wrote on it their opinion about this ruling criminal, and expressed their homage to Christ. Then they decided to smash the head of the statue of the greatest murderer in history, who killed countless millions of innocent men, women and children in his lust for power. The Secret Police were alarmed. They declared it a "terrorist act"and demanded that the children: "Denounce the criminal! If not, all 150 of you will be shot."

Zoia Leshtsheva came forward: "I alone have done it. Why should Stalin have a head if he never had loving, righteous, compassionate thoughts?" She had a special blessing promised by God to children of faithful parents. She was sentenced to death at the age of fourteen. Her sentence was changed to ten years of prison, to which another term was added, and then another. Her parents and brethren were freed long before she, but she continued to enjoy God's blessing in prison.

Pupils of a Soviet high school in Vilnus were taken to the Museum of Atheism. There, a lecturer showed them an ancient crucifix and explained, "This is a symbol of Christian superstition. The Christians irrationally believe that a certain Jesus was the Son of God, that He came down from heaven to die on a cross to atone for the sins we have committed, and to open for us the gates of paradise, which we Communists know does not exist."

A girl exclaimed in tears, "This is what I need. I need Jesus. I will love Him." The atheist had brought her to Christ.

Below are two letters written by Soviet Christian children to their mothers in prison for their faith:

God bless you, dear Mummy. Sincere greetings from your loving daughter. Don't be troubled by our temporary separation; the mischief is not eternal. Joy will hasten to come back. It will give courage to our family and to your heart. Now you know prison. Little Mummy, I can't imagine the feast we will have when you return. I do my lessons. Now it is evening. Tomorrow it will be morning. So day after day. And one day your release will come. I embrace you.

Another little girl:

Dear mother, when you come home, I will not think any more about solitude and pain. I made a poem for you:

You have a heart of gold,
You're young at heart, not old.
The Lord observes you from on high.
We'll be together soon, you and I.

I beg you not to weep, though I realize that prison will leave marks on your memory. Your loving daughter.

The Christians who die in prison leave behind children who eat from garbage, stuffing potato peels and stale bread crusts into their mouths with feverish fingers. But these children have learned from their fathers an earnest faith. The Moscow atheist magazine Nauka i Religia describes them: "In Kislovodsk, I spoke after a religious service with a girl of eleven. She was sincerely convinced that while she prays the good Lord looks at her and smiles. She says, 'There is God; I see Him myself. I believe no one who says He does not exist.' Another little girl kissed an image of Jesus crucified. Then she made her doll kiss it, too. When asked why, she said, 'God looked at the doll. I saw it.'

The magazine continues to tell us what Iurii, a boy of twelve, says: 'In my prayers, I ask God to give me strength to fight those who are against God. We have to fight them not with the sword, but with the Bible.' Another boy of the same age says, 'I ask God to forgive my sins, to make me strong, and that there should be no evil in me.'

Some years ago we received an open letter from two "small orphan children in the Lord," Shura and Galia Sloboda:

> *Dear children of God, we, your small sisters in the Lord, have been separated from our dear mother and father and two little sisters and a baby brother, although we are still very young. We have been taken away from them through the People's Court in the Verchedvinskii region, district of Vitebsk, because our dear ones taught us salvation in the name of our Lord Jesus Christ . . .*
>
> *We have been put in the orphanage of Vitebsk We cannot endure to be away from them, and we have therefore fled home twice, but the mighty of this world have again and again snatched us away from our family and placed us in the orphanage. Every day, we kneel by the side of our beds and pray for you all. And for this, we are terrorized and they always threaten to send us to a labor camp.*
>
> *On December 24, we felt urged to write to Moscow and complain about all threats and persecutions. We demanded to be allowed home during the winter holidays. Moscow gave their permission. But, alas, mother was no longer home! She had been sentenced to loss of freedom for four years because she had witnessed about Jesus Christ. Father received us together with our younger sisters and baby brother. He consoled us for a long time and said that Christians who love their Lord very much, have to walk on a heavy path.*
>
> *Dear mothers and fathers, who have consolation in the Lord, when you gather in your happy families, remember us when it is well with you. We ask you*

always in your meetings to carry us before our Almighty God in prayer, so that we can endure also this hard blow in our young lives and even unto death remain faithful in our hearts and trust in our Lord, who loves all.

The faithfulness of little children in Communist countries is often amazing. The son of someone named Ilyinov declared before court, "I will kill nobody. I will not, and that is final." Another child, Lilia Skomorokhova, declared, "I cannot be a member of the Pioneers [Communist children's organization]. Believers can't be members. Mummy told me she wishes to meet me in the other world. Communists don't get there."

A communication smuggled out of the Soviet Union told of the Baptist children Vania Vasiliev, Nadia Zdorova, and others between eight and fourteen years of age who were lured or intimidated by the Communist prosecutor Skrortshov into signing statements giving the names of the teachers of their Sunday school. As a result, four leading Christians of the town of Saki have been sentenced. Their conscience will brand these children forever as Judases; but, of course, at their age they did not realize they were being entrapped.

Also in the Soviet Union, the children of the Baptist family named Vidish were forcibly put in a home for mentally sick children, only because they believed in Christ. After one year of suffering there, they were abducted by their parents, who succeeded in bringing them into another town where doctors found them to be normal. But will the souls of these children ever recover from what they suffered?

What characterized the literature printed secretly by Christians in Russia was first of all its great care for the children. For instance, the following story appeared. Sister Mary L. had five children: Vania, Pavlik, Andrei, Vera, and Sveta. She bought them a rubber doll. But when the children played "prayer meeting," the knees of this doll could not be bent. So the children complained to their mother that she had bought them "an unbelieving doll."

Believers are recognized by the fact that they bend their knees before the Creator.

Believing children who are taught in school that the cosmonauts did not see God in space have answered: "But did the cosmonauts have a pure heart? Without it you will never see God, wherever you travel. With it, you can see Him everywhere!"

In this secret literature smuggled out of Russia, parents were asked to teach their children to be able to prove in school the existence of God. The leaflets maintained that Christian children in Russia "amaze lecturers and teachers by their steadfastness and religious heroism."

PART 9

CHINA AND OTHER LANDS

~52~

A FLOWER IN JESUS' GARDEN

RMANDO VALLADARES IS A CUBAN CHRISTIAN poet who was kept in jail for twenty-two years. After gaining his freedom, he published his memoirs. In them he described the horrors that took place in these Cuban jails, where there were more than 15,000 prisoners held on religious and political charges. A prisoner of only twelve was put in a cell with criminals. They bound him naked, laid him on his belly, and raped him. (In Russia, too, the brethren Tchemodanov and Klassen were put in cells with homosexuals.) In Cuban jails prisoners were beaten to a pulp. The jail had a large tank containing feces and urine. Prisoners were forced to stand up to the neck in this filth.

It would seem that under such conditions only one law could work: self-preservation at the expense of belief. But Christians have "laws different from all other peoples."

A believer named Geraldo, every time beatings started, shouted unceasingly, "Father, forgive them for they don't know what they do." He was shot while praying this prayer.

Valladares was once in the prison yard. An officer asked him, "Where do you get your power to resist? Why do you endure all this instead of giving up?" He plucked a flower, showed it to the

Communist, and said, "Before there were men on earth, there were flowers. When Capitalism and Communism are long since forgotten, the flowers will still be there. Our Holy Book compares the faithful with flowers. It is written, 'As the lily among thorns, so is my love among the daughters' (Song of Songs 2:2). Try to be a flower in Jesus' garden, and you will live forever."

From that moment, the officer became a different man. He no longer persecuted believers.

We can learn from such brethren to overcome the sorrows of our own lives.

~53~

ALWAYS TURN TO
WHAT IS HARDEST

*L*ENIN, FOUNDER OF MODEM INTERNATIONAL Communism, was a man who hated God. At the age of sixteen, he became upset by a stupid remark of a priest he overheard talking to his father: "If your son does not go to church willingly, beat him." Lenin tore off the cross he wore around his neck. As often happens, an incident that was really a trifle created in him a complex of antipathy toward religion. He confounded one wrong utterance of a priest with all the realities for which the notion "priest" stands: God, the Bible, eternal life. Then Holbach became his favorite philosopher, and he would later recommend strongly the wide dissemination of the writings of Holbach to the masses. He liked this philosopher, who had written, "God is my personal enemy."

What a small, seemingly insignificant incident led Lenin to become an atheist! It might be useful to note how Sigmund Freud, the renowned psychiatrist, also became an atheist. In his childhood, Freud had greatly admired his father, looking upon him as a hero. When Sigmund was seven, his father told him that he had been attacked once by a gang that shouted: "Down from the pavement, you dirty Jew! Jews should walk in the middle of the street." They also threw his cap in the mud.

The child asked, "Daddy, what did you do then?"

The father replied, "I grabbed the cap and left the pavement."

That was obviously the right thing to do when dealing with a gang. Heroism is a rare virtue that should not be squandered on minor incidents. But the father did not explain this to Sigmund, and the boy could not have been expected to understand. From that moment on Freud despised and hated his father. This hatred, which began with so small a reason, grew to the point where he dreamed of killing his father. When he matured, he extended his hatred to all fathers. He wrote a book against Moses because he was the father of the Jewish people. Freud also wrote against God, the Father of the universe.

Do our socalled convictions also have trifles as their origin?

Vietnam, Cuba, and above all China, still apply strictly Lenin's principle:

> Terror must be perpetrated unmercifully and in the shortest time possible, because people cannot endure continued cruelty of the regime; the trials must be conducted promptly, ending in swift sentences for the greatest number of clergy.
>
> The confiscation of monasteries and churches should be carried out with the greatest severity, without scruples and in the shortest possible time; the more priests executed during this occasion, the better.

Such adamant terror can be broken only by adamant faithfulness. Lukewarm Christians cannot resist. Elect souls, whom it is good to imitate, should follow the teaching of John of the Cross: "Turn always to what is hardest, not to what is easy; to what is most distasteful, not to what tastes best; to labor not to rest; to what is lowest and most contemptible, not to the highest and most precious."

Christians in such countries know they must propagate the gospel without counting the cost. We must do the same in our own circumstances.

Great persecution still rages in Vietnam. In the Filipino monthly Impact, the Jesuit priest F. Gomez, who spent fifteen years in Vietnamese jails, described the power of darkness behind this persecution. He had a discussion with a high-ranking Communist official from Hanoi, who told him, "We do not admit the heresy of pluralism, because this means division and weakness. We care only about the people." He immediately added an explanation of what he meant: "People" are only those who have the correct ideology and live according to it. There are some stubborn, hard-headed people like Archbishop Thuan. These will never become "people." He also told the priest, "Nobody will come out of the concentration camp until he is converted to Communism. Those who do not convert will disappear." When the priest asked if Communists would grant religious freedom, the Communist official answered, "Freedom exists so that you can obey, in different ways, the rules of the Communist Party."

Shocked by the Communist's frankness, the Jesuit said to him, "I am a foreigner who can leave the country. If I repeat what you have said in the free world, it will certainly be bad propaganda for Communism."

The Communist answered, "Priest, no one will believe you."

The wicked are adamant in wickedness. We will be conquerors only if we are adamant in our goodness.

~54~

EXEMPLARY CHINESE GIRLS

*I*N KIANGSI, RED CHINA, A PASTOR AND TWO
Christian girls were sentenced to death. As on
many other occasions in church history, the persecutors mocked them. They promised to release the pastor if he
would shoot the girls. He accepted. The girls waited in the
prison yard for the announced execution. A fellow-prisoner who
watched the scene from his prison cell described their faces as
pale but beautiful beyond belief, infinitely sad but sweet.
Humanly speaking, they were fearful, but determined to submit
to death rather than renounce their faith. Flanked by guards, the
executioner came with a revolver in his hand: it was their pastor.

He told them about the deal he had struck with the
Communists and how wise it had been to do so. They would
have died in any case, but so would he. Is it not better that a
pastor should remain alive? The girls whispered to each other,
then bowed respectfully before the pastor. One of them said, in
effect:

> *Before being shot by you, we wish to thank you*
> *heartily for what you have meant to us. You baptized*
> *us, you taught us the way of eternal life, you gave us*

Holy Communion with the same hand in which you
now hold the gun. May God reward you for all the
good you have done us. You also taught us that
Christians are sometimes weak and commit terrible
sins, but they can be forgiven again. When you regret
what you are about to do to us, do not despair like
Judas, but repent like Peter. God bless you. And
remember that our last thought was not one of indig-
nation against your failure. Everyone passes through
hours of darkness. We die with gratitude.

They bowed again. The pastor's heart was hardened beyond repentance. He shot the girls. Immediately afterwards he was shot by the Communists.

Life often creates conflicts between people, though not always as dramatic as that just recounted. Let us learn from these martyrs how to meet the betrayal of friendships and the unfaithfulness of those in whom we have confided. Another episode from Red China: A girl was put through much torture to get her to betray the secrets of the Underground Church. She was asked how she could bear so much suffering.

She replied:

It was not hard. I had been taught by my pastor that
the real torture lasts very little. For one minute of
torture, there are ten minutes of glancing at the
enraged faces and the implements of pain. I decided
to keep my eyes closed the whole time. I did not see the
stick before it hit me, nor afterward. The suffering
was much reduced. I relied on the promise of Christ:
"Blessed are the pure in heart, for they shall see God"
(Matthew 5: 8). I purified my heart of fear of men,
and I learned to see God. Just so, many had seen Him
before. When the Communists became aware of my
defense, they stuck my eyelids open with tape, but it
was too late. My vision had already taken on a new
aspect.

RICHARD WURMBRAND

55

IDENTIFYING WITH CHRIST

*I*F A MAN STOOD BY A ROADSIDE AND WATCHED the whole population of China walk past him at the rate of one individual per second, more than twenty years would elapse before the last member of the procession went by. The strictest Leninism rules these people. Lenin wrote, "Everything is moral that is necessary for the annihilation of the old exploiting order." According to Lenin, religion belongs in this category. It must be obliterated.

But Christians in China trust death. It is the way to enter into the embraces of the heavenly Bridegroom and to receive the holy kiss. A strange report comes from the province of Hunan. A preacher was hanged by the Communists, but they left too quickly. The brethren were able to cut him down, and he is still alive. He says that when the rope was around his neck and he was being hauled up over the branch of a tree, all he could think of was our Lord being raised up on the Cross. A Christian poem by Radu Gyn was smuggled out of a Romanian prison. It is characteristic of the belief of the Underground Church. Here are its main thoughts:

Last night, Jesus entered my cell. How sad, how tall was Christ.

He stood near my bed and said, "Put your hand on my wounds."

He had on His ankles marks and rust, as if He had once borne chains. I arose from under my gray blanket, "Lord, whence, from what age, do you come?" Jesus put a finger to His mouth and made me a sign to be silent. When I awoke from sleep, the straw smelled like roses. But Jesus was no more there. I shouted through iron bars, "Where are You, Lord?" Then I saw in my own hands the marks of His nails.

The Underground Church bears in its body the marks of Christ. Whoever blesses her blesses Him. Whoever helps her helps Him. Whoever learns from her learns from Him. Let us learn from these overcomers of the world!

~56~

AN ARAB GIRL

ARY KHOURY WAS SEVENTEEN WHEN Damour, her village in Lebanon, was raided by Muslim fanatics bent on converting everyone to Islam by force. She and her parents were confronted with one choice: "If you do not become a Muslim, you will be shot."

She knew Jesus had been given a similar choice: "Give up your plan of saving sinners or you will be crucified." He chose the Cross. Therefore she replied, "I was baptized as a Christian and His word came to me: 'Don't deny your faith.' I will obey Him. Go ahead and shoot." A young man did so, and left her for dead. Two days later, the Red Cross came into her village. Mary, alone of her family, was found alive, but the bullet had severed her spinal cord.

She was now a paraplegic. Her paralyzed arms were stretched out and bent at the elbows, reminiscent of Christ at His crucifixion

But words from the Lord had come to her. She knew what she must do with her handicapped life. "Everyone has a vocation," she said. "I can never marry or do any physical work. So I will offer my life for Muslims, like the one who cut my father's throat, stabbed my mother while cursing her, and tried to kill me. My life will be a prayer for them."

Such prayers shattered Communism, as billions spent on nuclear weapons could never do. They will also bring Muslims to the Son of God. Therese of Lisieux said, "Sufferings gladly borne for others convert more people than sermons."

Mary's example encouraged other Christians to take a heroic stand. During 1990, the fiercest year of the fifteen year Lebanese civil war, 1,000 were killed, 3,000 wounded and 300,000 fled the country—among them missionaries whose duty should have been to stay with their flock. But some remained. Luciem Accad, director of the Bible Society, stayed on, though a family of five was killed next door and a shell exploded in his own home, sending a wall crashing down on him. The blast left him deaf in one ear, but the other is enough for him to use in spreading God's word.

His spirit was good. "People are coming to the Lord every day," he reported.

-57-

CHINESE HEROES OF FAITH

ON HIS DEATHBED, GENERAL BOOTH, THE founder of the Salvation Army, told his son Bramwell, "Take the gospel to China." Years ago I wrote that if I were on my deathbed, I would say, "Take the gospel to the Communist camp." This wish has been fulfilled.

In China, under the terror of Mao, some Christians prayed in whispers with their wives to avoid telling about their faith to the children lest they speak about it in school. But others formed secret house churches that eventually mushroomed. When Mao came to power in 1949 there were 3.5 million Christians in China. Now the Protestants alone are said to number 70 million.

During the time of the fiercest terror, Sister Kwang organized small groups of itinerant evangelists who went from place to place forming small congregations. Her twelve-year-old son was beaten by the Red Guards till he died. She and her husband were publicly whipped, yet refused to deny Christ. In jail she volunteered to clean toilets in order to be able to circulate and tell fellow-prisoners about Christ, bringing many to conversion. Freed for a time "Mother Kwang," as she was called by friends and co-workers, created about 300 congregations, some with thousands of members. In 1974, she was sentenced to lifelong imprisonment, tortured, and put in an underground cell with only a bucket for sanitary needs as furniture. Since it was rarely emptied, Mother Kwang was plagued with lice and mosquitoes. Her only food was unwashed rice full of sand. Freed after more than a decade in prison, she continued to live by laws "different from all other people's," including those who seek peace by conforming to the whims of tyrants.

In Mao's time, in a Chudse hospital, it was required that each morning everyone kowtow to Mao's image. One doctor remembered the three Jews of old who allowed themselves to be thrown into a burning fiery furnace rather than yield to idolatry, so he refused. For this he was beaten daily. While being beaten he sang, "Who shall separate us from the love of Christ? Trouble, distress, persecution?" The Communists beat him with a rope, a metal rod, and a heavy cudgel, yet God's consolation was greater than the suffering. He did not bow.

Then they tried to break him by making his wife and seven children attend his tortures. His wife pleaded, "What will our children do if you die? For our sake, please do as they demand!" But this Chinese doctor knew the teaching of Jesus: "If anyone comes to me and does not hate his father and mother, wife and children, brothers and sisters, yes, and his own life also, he cannot be my disciple" (Luke 14:26).

From the experience of the universal Church throughout the centuries, he could expect some of his children to be traumatized for life and even to doubt forever his parental love. He could also expect that they would follow their father's example if they were God's elect, and in time become heroic believers ready to sacrifice themselves. The Communists hung the doctor up to be beaten, and poked hot irons in his face. On another occasion he was stripped naked and forced to stand on a bench in freezing weather. The Lord who protected the three worthies in the furnace protected him in the cold. He survived and remained faithful. For such a one, God becomes the supreme desire and no sacrifice is too great.

A Church with such heroes of the faith has power, as the following story indicates.

In Red China, someone wanted to rape a girl on her way home from a house church, where she had received teachings on love and forgiveness. When she was grabbed, she did not scream, kick, or run. She had been taught to love assailants and to see in them men who have to be brought to salvation. With all meekness, she asked her would—be rapist for permission to pray before he fulfilled his sinful desire. It was granted. She knelt and prayed loudly. There must have been flames of love in this prayer, because when she opened her eyes and arose from kneeling, the rapist was also kneeling, though unable to move. He had become paralyzed. She ran back to the church to tell what had happened. The elders said she must forgive the man (she already understood this) and pray for his healing. As a result, he was restored, and all the non-Christians in her village turned to Christ.

According to another report, two Chinese Christians were led to torture and death. One quoted Jesus' words "it is finished" in a whisper. His brother answered, "No, that's not what Jesus said when He suffered. He said, "It is accomplished."

Our brethren and sisters in China were terribly tortured by having water forced up the nose, by having their hands crushed with wood between the knuckles, and by severe electric shocks. Only those who love Christ supremely can resist such inhumanity.

~58~

A SHORT AND LIGHT AFFLICTION

OBODY IS THE SAME PERSON AFTER MEETING John Jue Han Ding. He is a Chinese pastor who went to Tibet to preach the gospel. For this he was arrested by the Communists and spent twenty years in prison. In him I met a being such as I had never met before. To look into his shining face, to hear the heavenly music coming from his mouth, to get acquainted with his story, enlarged my knowledge of dedication and holiness.

I felt like a botanist discovering in some virgin forest a flower of exquisite beauty, previously completely unknown.

The tortures he endured are beyond description. It is enough to say that at a certain moment they tied his hands behind his back and then emptied a bucket of human waste on his head. He was kept like that for days, without being given any opportunity to clean himself. He was given food, but with his hands tied behind his back he had to lie on the floor and lick it up like an animal. The food had to pass through soiled lips. He still did not deny his faith and refused to admit to crimes he had not committed.

Then his torturers filled a cell with human waste and put him in it with a multitude of common criminals. Now they all waded and suffocated in it. The common criminals were told they would all be kept like this indefinitely unless they forced him to comply with the demands of the interrogators. To survive, these criminals now competed in torturing him day and night. When he came to this point in his story, John Jue Han Ding passed from speaking to singing, with a beautiful voice and an ecstatic face, a text from one of Paul's epistles: "For our light affliction, which is but for a moment, works for us a far more exceeding and eternal weight of glory; while we look not at the things which are seen, but at the things which are not seen: for the things which are seen are temporal; but the things which are not seen are eternal" (2 Corinthians 4:17-18).

How heavy our light afflictions seem, and how light for him were the afflictions that we would consider were the heaviest imaginable. In John Jue Han Ding's life we see a saint passing through the deepest pits of suffering and reaching the greatest heights of inner peace.

Are such beings only human?

In the Hebrew of 1 Samuel 10:22, which refers to Saul the future king of the Jews, a big white space is left in the middle of the sentence after the word Ish, which stands for "man." Rabbis explain it as showing that Saul, receiving the Spirit from above, has become more than a man. The opportunity has been given to him to reach heavenly heights.

This happened in the case of our Chinese brother.

People are seldom forced to endure cruelties like those he suffered. But everyone has cause for sadness or is acquainted with others in deep sorrow. We can point them to God, to Christ. But it is also very effective to point them to contemporary Christlike exemplars of heroism. Ding refused to the end to sign what the Communists demanded of him, thus demonstrating that one can successfully withstand any evil. Some men are unbreakable, more than conquerors. Under exceptional circumstances Jue Han Ding remained firm. We can take

RICHARD WURMBRAND

courage from his fortitude so that we too can be more than conquerors.

I believe it is very profitable to see Christ in the lives of His saints.

Christ is eternally selfexistent and omnipresent.

Amshel Rothschild was not a Christian. Tso-Po-Tao lived before Christ came to this earth. They too belonged to the soul of His Church, striving after what is noble, true, beautiful, and loving even without knowing Him. It is written that on the eighth day His parents gave the Savior the name "Jesus." The shepherds in Bethlehem and the Magi believed in Him without knowing this most holy name.

PART 10

THE GOSPEL NET

-59-

WORKING WITH A
SENSE OF URGENCY

*T*HE ORTHODOX JEWS OF JESUS' TIME WERE
extremely reluctant to allow any work to be done
on the seventh day of the week. The Sabbath was
a day for worshiping in the temple. Jesus no doubt startled them
by asking, "Which of you shall have an ass or an ox fallen into
a pit, and will not straightway pull him out on the Sabbath
day?" (Luke 14:5).

At first glance, many words of Jesus seem to us childishly
simple to understand, and we marvel why His contemporaries
had difficulty with their meaning. Jesus healed several sick
people on the Sabbath and, as if this were not enough to upset
the religious authorities, He even commanded one of them to
carry his own bed during the Sabbath day. While those around
Him may have wondered why healing could not be postponed
another day, since these people had been sick for years, Jesus
treated the afflicted as total emergencies. He illustrated the same
urgency on other occasions. When the Jews were upset that His
disciples plucked and ate ears of corn on the Sabbath day, Jesus
compared their action to King David's. When fleeing in great

haste from Saul's wrath he ate of the consecrated temple bread (Matthew 12:3).

If we look superficially, like the Jews of Jesus' time, we too will fail to perceive the urgency. Why not postpone by one day the healing of a condition that existed for many years, or the carrying of one's bed? What could this hurry have to do with Jesus' spiritual message on earth?

The falling of an ox into a well or pit was indeed a dire emergency that would not have allowed its owner to have an easy day. In fact, it might have wrecked more than the Sabbath, and perhaps his whole livelihood. A drowned ox was a big loss, for it was the animal used to pull the plow and thus obtain a crop of wheat to feed the family.

The donkey was used for transportation and for carrying loads. Its falling into a well must have been, in those times, a bigger disaster than wrecking a car nowadays. Also, how long could a family survive without water? The situation could not be ignored or postponed.

There is no step-by-step procedure on how to hoist an ox out of a narrow well, yet great skill is needed. It is difficult to get an ass moving even on a straight road, let alone climbing or backing out of a well. The carrot and stick would be useless as threats. The one suffering the loss would try all orthodox and unorthodox methods, use all approved and unapproved, pleasant and unpleasant means in order to get his animal out, in whatever shape.

There is no indication as to how much time or financial and emotional effort the task would take. The owner would work frantically against time and most likely alone, for the place is narrow. Such a disaster occurs suddenly. A small slip and the damage is done.

Those who don't know Jesus live without knowing real life. Lives without Jesus are irremediably lost. In such cases, one should not be choosy about the means of rescue.

The work of spreading the gospel where it is forbidden or hindered must be treated as an emergency.

RICHARD WURMBRAND

The Greek word *eutheos*, translated in Luke 14:5 as "straight-away" [immediately], is the most characteristic word of Mark's Gospel. It is found more often in Mark than in all the other Gospels combined. The reason is as follows. Tradition identifies Mark as the rich man to whom Jesus said that in order to be perfect he should sell everything he had and give to the poor. It seemed to him at that time too big a price, and he left the place with sadness. Later he repented and fulfilled the commandment of the Lord, but there remained remorse in his heart for the time lost in disobedience. Therefore he repeats continually in his Gospel the word *eutheos*—straightaway.

What is good must be done straightaway, immediately. Only this moment is ours. The next moment might belong to death, even if we are young and in perfect health. If we don't act immediately, other cares might make us forget our duty. So if our hearts are moved by the suffering of our fellow-believers, wherever they might be today, let us act on our convictions and loving impulses. Tomorrow may be too late. Those who work with such a sense of urgency make a great impact.

A report out of China revealed how Christianity spread in that repressive society:

> *Ten brothers and sisters [in Christ] were imprisoned, beaten and bound. They regarded their sufferings for the Lord as more precious than the treasures of Egypt. They had preached with tears streaming down, causing the passersby and street-sellers, Christians and non-Christians, to stand still and listen. Even the fortune tellers were moved by the Holy Spirit and burst out crying. Many people hearing the Word forgot to eat, work, or even return home. The brothers and sisters preached until they were exhausted, but the crowd would not let them leave. The authorities, however, came and dragged the Christians away one by one, binding them with ropes and beating them with electric-shock poles, knocking them unconscious.*

But when they revived, they continued to pray, sing, and preach to the bystanders.

When they were bound and beaten, many people noticed a strange expression on their faces, and the crowd saw to their amazement that they were smiling. Their spirit and appearance were so lively and gracious that many were led to believe in Jesus by their example. When the brothers and sisters in that area saw them bound and forced to kneel on the ground for more than three days without food or water, and beaten with sticks until their faces were covered with blood, with their hands made black by the ropes—but still praying, singing and praising the Lord—then they too wished to share persecution. So in this area recently the flame of the gospel has spread everywhere.

In men's eyes this is an unfortunate happening, but for Christians it is like a rich banquet. This lesson cannot be learned from books, and this sweetness is not usually tasted by men. This rich life does not exist in a comfortable environment. Where there is no cross, there is no crown. If the spices are not refined to become oil, the fragrance of the perfume cannot flow forth; and if the grapes are not crushed in the vat, they will not become wine.

"Dear brethren," concludes the one who recounted this incident, "these saints who have gone down into the furnace, far from being harmed, have had their faces glorified."

~60~

CHRIST OUTSIDE THE CHURCH

*W*ITHOUT CHURCHES AND WITHOUT BIBLES, people in the Communist camp have suffered from a thirst for God. So they find Him outside church buildings.

In a capital city I once entered the tourist agency of a Communist country. When I told them my identity, they immediately called their embassy. The embassy sent over a representative, and I had before me four Communists, considered trustworthy enough to be sent abroad. I told them about Christ. Instead of the expected words of opposition, the one from the embassy told me, "Pastor, I dreamed one night that I was in a meadow. Jesus was also there and caressed my head. Why should I have dreamt about Him? I did not believe in Him. And why should Jesus have caressed an atheist? The whole of the next day I was in a kind of ecstasy. Could you explain to me what this means?"

What an opportunity for a pastor! I used it to good advantage.

"The most High dwelleth not in temples made with hands; as saith the prophet" (Acts 7:48). What a shock these words must have been for the Jews of old. Each year they traveled from countries far away or hundreds of miles in their own country to fulfill the obligation, imposed by their religious laws, of making frequent pilgrimages to Jerusalem. When they arrived at the Temple to meet God, the words of the prophet were read to them: "The Most High does not dwell in temples made by hands." Where then can man find God? And what are temples for if God is not in them?

Temples serve to point to the first real tabernacle, which the will of the Most High placed in a manger in a stable among cattle. God came to "tabernacle" with men as a baby, in whom dwelt all the fullness of the Godhead bodily. In the New Jerusalem the prophet John "saw no temple, for the Lord God Almighty and the Lamb are the temple of it" (Revelation 21:22).

The Communists, of course, do not know this. They believed that by destroying churches they would destroy people's belief in God. But God can speak to an atheist in his bedroom.

One Russian Orthodox priest, Serghei Zheludkov of Pskov, publicly aligned himself with Pavel Litvinov, a Russian freedom-fighter, sentenced because he protested against the invasion of Czechoslovakia by the Soviet Union. Zheludkov wrote him a wonderful letter:

> I heard that you are an atheist. This does not hinder my admiration for you . . . The Church, the mystical body of Christ, consists of men of good will and action, independent of their so-called "convictions. " As a healthy cell of a living body may know nothing about the head of the body, about the whole body, so a man of good will may be "an unbeliever, " may not know and not think about Christ, about God—and, notwithstanding, belong to the Church of Christ. Today in Russia many call themselves atheists only because of lack of education . . . Love, liberty, truth, fearlessness, loyalty, all these are names of our Lord,

whom you honor not knowing Him, and whom you preached in your wonderful courageous attitudes.

Some of these ideas may seem strange to Western Christians. But I know of a young Russian scientist who, on a visit to the United States, was asked about religious persecution in Russia. He answered very sincerely, "We have to put many Christians in prison, because at their religious services they cut off the hands and legs of children as a sacrifice to God." He had been taught such things about Christianity.

If this were all I knew about Christianity, I would be antiChristian, too!

-61-

CHAIN LETTERS

*I*N A SOVIET NEWSPAPER, MOLODIOJ GRUZII, WE learned about the sentencing of three Orthodox Christians: Kasimov, Matchalov and Abramishvili. They had committed the crime of organizing the sending of chain letters.

Since this was a specific Soviet crime unknown in the free world, we should explain. Unable to publish the gospel or print Christian books, our brethren decided to write longhand or typewritten letters with many carbon copies—they have no copy machines—and send them to addresses picked from the telephone book, or else to put them in mailboxes. Those who received the letters were then asked in turn to multiply and distribute them by the same means. Thus they reached far corners of the Soviet Union. The work began in the Caucasus, but Ukrainian newspapers indicated that such letters circulated in their republic, too.

The letter for which our brethren went to prison started with "Our Father," the meaning of which people in the Soviet Union would not know if it were not for such chain letters. Then it continued: "Atheists are the helpers of antichrist. Have no fellowship with them . . . The 'paradise' that atheists and their government have created on earth is deceptive. The antichrists buy men with movies and other amusements and lead them astray with godless teachings . . . They take our children and put them into kindergartens and schools that are incubators without love. There they destroy faith in God. They become harsh, thieves, drunkards." The letter finishes with the appeal, "Pray; ask grace from God, forgiveness, and protection."

These letters were of special importance to Soviet children who were not allowed to attend religious services. They were an important means of instructing them in the faith. It was not a question of just a few letters. The newspaper informed us that the Christians flooded the town of Tbilisi with their writings.

Another newspaper, Molodioj Moldavii, spoke of "an offensive on the part of the believers." After fifty years of bloody tyranny, the atheists of the Soviet Union were on the defensive. One of the weapons with which Christians defeated the Communists, who had at their disposal all the schools, publishing houses, radio and television stations, plus prisons and instruments of torture, were these simple chain letters!

I call upon readers of this book to use similar weapons. The Church was never meant to be an organization in which a few do the work and the others contribute money.

We are all to be part of the priesthood of all believers, involved in the ministry of spreading the good news far and near.

~62~

Poet Risks Jail

*S*OLOUHIN, A RUSSIAN COMMUNIST, WAS BITTERLY attacked by his comrades for writing "wrong" poetry, which might have landed him in jail. One sees in his poems a primitive, unconscious groping for God, a seeking for what is holy without religious knowledge of any kind. They would not satisfy an American fundamentalist minister, who would find they did not correspond with his Bible and books of dogma, but would fail to see that because of his own failure to engage in secret missionary work in Russia, the young poet probably had never seen a Bible or any other Christian book.

In one poem, Solouhin describes an ancient Orthodox church, with holy images seemingly of burnished gold.

When evening came "in the church, even darkness somehow appeared to be golden."

How golden is even darkness when it is a church? This, only a Russian could tell you. Their churches have been taken away, therefore they value them. Westerners have churches on every corner, therefore they criticize them. They do not observe how golden are even the Churches' failures and sins, because there is always in the Church not only the human but also the divine.

One icon there, says Solouhin, is five centuries old. For 500 years the holy mother painted on it wept over her soon crucified Son, but also wept with all the sinners who bowed in church confessing their sins. Then the image was thrown on the rubbish heap. The church was transformed into an official building for the Soviets, where no one weeps with those who weep. The holy image was picked up by a farmer lady, who hung it in a place of honor in her home. On a visit to her village, Solouhin saw it and told the lady that she could get good money by selling it to some museum because of its value as an artistic antiquity. The farmer lady answered, "Cut me in pieces, burn out my eyes with red-hot irons. I will not give the mother of the Lord, the luminous Mary's picture, to be mocked by devils."

Solouhin finished his poem by telling us that for years he traveled without ever being able to forget the picture of the holy mother and the Holy Child in her lap.

The Russian publication Religion and Atheism in the Soviet Union reported the following:

A teacher, Mrs. Ziazeva, wrote to the newspapers and to the propagandists of atheism that, after studying the gospel, the Koran [holy book of the Muslims] and the Vedas [holy book of the Hindus], she came to Christianity in its Eastern Orthodox form because it gave light and warmth to her philosophical search.

The Soviet historian, Anna Tihaia, returned her membership card to the Komsomol, the Communist youth organization, because it is atheistic. When interrogated, she explained that she arrived at her belief in God after having thought critically about the contemporary science of official materialism. She could not remain a university professor. She became an unqualified worker in a factory and a Baptist activist.

The gospel survived in other Communist countries as well, even among the ruling class. When the Soviets entered Czechoslovakia the members of the Czech Parliament, surrounded by Russian troops, were in panic. Only one member, a Christian, quietly took out his Bible and read. The others asked him, "Don't you care about the tragedy around us?

We ourselves might be arrested and deported to Siberia soon. How can you sit so quietly?"

He answered, "This is the Word of God, which gives comfort to the troubled heart."

They then invited him to read the Scriptures from the rostrum of the Communist Parliament, from which only bitter Leninist theories had been propagated. Later sixty members of parliament asked for Bibles and received them.

~63~

LENIN'S ALLEGED CONVERSION

*I*N JUNE OF 1926, OSSERVATORE ROMANO, official organ of the Vatican, published an account claiming that the Hungarian priest Vittorio Bodo, friend of Lenin from the time of his youth as an emigrant in the West, visited him when he was fatally ill.

Lenin allegedly told the priest, "I have erred. No doubt many oppressed had to be freed, but our method has provoked other oppressions and horrible massacres. My mortal grief is to be immersed in an ocean of blood of innumerable victims. It is too late to turn back, though what we would have needed in order to save Russia was ten St. Francis' of Assisi."

Monsignor D'Herbigny, bishop of Ilio, doubted the story and so spoke personally with the priest Bodo and had it confirmed from his mouth. He told about this encounter in a lecture published in an Italian magazine in 1946.

Lenin had been under Christian influence. His wife Krupskaia wrote in her memoirs that he had met the Orthodox priest Gapon, later hanged by the Communists. But most amazing is what Nauka i Religia, the Soviet atheist magazine, published in December 1973:

> *Lenin showed great interest in the writings of Christian sectarians, which a fellow Communist had gathered, especially in the old manuscripts. He studied them thoroughly . . . He was especially interested in their philosophical writings. Once after thoroughly reading the manuscripts of "the spiritual Molokani"* [a specific Russian sect, afterwards almost uprooted by the Communists], *he said, "How interesting. This has been created by simple people. Whole books. "*

The Communist magazine said that much. Who knows how much more was behind the story? Perhaps a deathbed conversion due to some primitive writings of old believers or due to some book about Francis of Assisi given to him by the priest Bodo. We don't know. Heaven is a place of surprises. We might be surprised to find there the converted mass-slaughterer of Christians, Vladimir Lenin. Some dissidents who emerged from the Soviet Union asserted that they knew Lenin had confessed to a priest before his death. His Christian victims sufered and died praying for him. Their prayers may very well have been accepted.

We have always urged people to write to Communist leaders and to left-wing personalities in our own country, as well as to leaders in the free world. In Judah, "the princes went in to the king in the court . . . and told all the words of Jeremiah the prophet in the ears of the king" (Jeremiah 36:20). We should catch big fish for Christ!

Malenkov, who was first co-worker and successor to Stalin and collaborated in the killing of millions of innocents, died a born-again Christian. His conversion came about one day when he, the privileged Communist ruler who enjoyed all the luxuries of life, took it upon himself to join poor citizens who were waiting in a long line to get bread. A slave master wanted to find out how it was to feel the other end of the whip. The KGB officers Ataiev and I. Konnikov, after torturing many Christians, died as Christian martyrs themselves. They came to the Savior by bowing over their victims to try to feel how it was to be tortured.

If we practice faith consistently as our persecuted brethren do, we will also acquire enormous spiritual power and will be able to overcome seemingly invincible enmity.

PART 11

LETTERS FROM MARTYRS

-64-

EXTRAORDINARY CHRISTMAS GREETINGS

CHRISTMAS LETTER SMUGGLED OUT OF THE Soviet Union arrived in the West after much delay. It was written by the Russian Christian writer Alexander Petrov-Agatov, who had spent a total of thirty years in prisons and concentration camps for his faith before being released. This letter is a gem of love. Read it carefully:

> *On Christmas Eve I remember all men, independent of their faith and color of their social position or level of education. I remember men in power and those who suffer in jails and camps, the rich and the poor, the strong and the weak, those who have risen to peaks and those who have fallen into the abyss, the sick and the healthy, the persecuted and the persecutors. Foremost, I think about those whom I only recently left after having been with them in prison and camps for almost thirty years.*
>
> *On our festive table there is a small Christmas tree: apples, grapes and other dainties. In my heart words ring like a bell—can you eat all these things while at least one man is hungry? Can you sleep in a warm bed when somewhere a prisoner is not allowed to lie down even on the cold concrete?*

Garlands ornament my Christmas tree while the heavy chains of slavery and barbed wire surround the camps. I do not write only about Soviet camps and prisons. I think also about those who have no freedom in other countries. I think about all those who do not eat and drink this night, who cannot look at the most sparkling star which made Christ known to the wise men because the prison windows are covered with planks.

I greet, on Christmas day, our eagles and doves— mothers and wives, brides and those who could not become brides—my sisters who take the cross for the word of God, for truth, for righteousness, for faithfulness toward God and love toward men.

Christmas greetings to all the persecuted, the suffering, to all those who seek light. Christmas greetings to all persecutors and oppressors, to all those who curse and confiscate.

Christmas greetings to Helen Zagriazkina, who betrayed me seven years ago. I visited the church in which you worshipped. I wished to see you face to face, but was told that you don't go there anymore. But do you ever pray? Pray, pray!

All men, prisoners and guards, men of the secret police and patrol officers, secretaries or the Communist central committees and presidents pray while it is not too late. There will be no second birth of Christ. There will be a second coming. "Behold, I come soon," says the Lord. Soon, very soon.

Reading such words of wisdom and love from one who has suffered thirty years of jail helps us value our sufferings. "Jesus, though He were a Son, yet learned His obedience by the things which He suffered" (Hebrews 5:8). Not favorable but unfavorable circumstances are the hammers that shape the saints of God. Only men and women of courage who throw themselves into depths of sorrow come up with pearls, not those who for the sake of comfort shun the sea and the waves.

-65-

THOSE WHOM POISON DOES NOT KILL

*I*N THE LIVES OF MANY PRISONERS, THE LORD'S promise is fulfilled: "If those who believe shall drink any deadly thing, it shall not hurt them" (Mark 16:18). The Communist Secret Police poison the prisoners slowly, sometimes putting drugs in their food, in order to break them morally and transform them through biological experiments into primitive creatures who will not think. But we have evidence to the contrary. I quote from a letter smuggled out of prison by the Soviet Christian David Klassen (remember, the following lines come from a prison cell):

> *At midnight I bowed my knee before God and thanked Him for all the graces which He has shown us. He has forgiven all our sins . . . He places us on the way of truth, He comforts us in our misery, in our suffering, in our separation . . . We will pray for the cleansing of the Christ's Church, that she may bring forth more fruit . . . We will pray for the ministers, for the youth, for the prisoners and their families, for our country and its government.*

From another letter written in prison:

> *Don't weep, soul, that griefs surround you. Your lot*
> *does not lie in earthly life. The whole of happiness is*
> *where the saints who finished their course on earth*
> *live peacefully. Yes, I was obliged to go this way. There*
> *is no other way for me as a minister. And if someone*
> *wishes to be a minister, he must know beforehand*
> *that, when the Jews entered into the Holy Land,*
> *crossing the Jordan, the priests entered first in the*
> *dangerous water and were the last to leave it.*

How much we who eat dainties can learn from these Christians fed with poisonous food!

The prophet Obadiah charged the Edomites, a people who lived 2,600 years ago at the east end of the Dead Sea, with participating in the sacking of Jerusalem and in the desecration of the temple. He said, "Ye have drunk upon my holy mountain" (Obadiah 1:16). The Communists have also changed many churches into cocktail bars. They have done even worse: they have changed churches into courthouses in which Christians are judged for their faith.

The Catholic priest Stephen Kurti was sentenced to death in Albania for having baptized a child. The trial took place in the former church of the town of Milot. The priest pleaded guilty and said, "I am a priest. It is my duty to give the sacraments." He left behind as his only property a radio.

-66-

Prison Letters

*W*HEN THERE WERE NO CARS, TRAINS, PLANES, phones, faxes, and all the gadgets that make modern life easier, people had time to write letters. Today a person who cultivates this art form is rare. We could well learn from the masters of life and love to write beautifully.

Over the years we have received many letters smuggled out of prisons. The letter that follows is representative.

> *Thank you for the parcel. The officers took counsel from each other several days on what to do with the parcel. Then in the end the order came that I could receive it on condition that I write back, "Please don't send parcels more than four times a year." I answered, "I can write this, but what the others will do I don't know."*
>
> *My beloved, I must confess that I miss nothing. The Lord has given me a good appetite so that I am satisfied even with the food which no pig would eat.* [That sentence should inspire us never to bicker about our food in the West.] *We are bent to the*

earth with gratitude that so many pray for us, as we have heard from you that it happens. Yes, our well-being depends on this . . .

My hair becomes gray. I have more and more wrinkles on my face. I have to work in great heat. My work is at an oven in which brooms are dried. I work 15 hours a day, from five in the evening until eight in the morning. During this time I have to be entirely naked, but still the sweat can be gathered with buckets from my body. You have to wipe yourself continually.

Is the oak in our garden still growing? ["Oak" was the nickname of one of the leaders of the Underground Church. In this way our brother was inquiring about the progress of the underground work.] *When I was a child, the percentage of Baptists among the active Christians of Russia was small. Now it has greatly increased.*

Here is another letter from a Christian prisoner in the Soviet Union.

The pressures which are used against us here and which are repugnant to the flesh, cause men to lose completely their honor and to become worse than animals. But these samZe thinzgs are useful and unavoidable, for those who love God, in becoming godly. Therefore we have no reason to complain.

Recently we were brought before a court. It was proposed that we walk crooked ways in order to have things better in the future. One of the judges said, "Is all the pain you have had to endure not enough to have produced in you a change of mind?"

I answered, "I have passed through no pains. Prison is a place in which I have learned very many good things, and which has made me more determined in my faith. You will not be able to understand this riddle because you don't believe in God. "

I will now be appointed as the gardener of the prison, and I would be very happy to receive from you some flower seeds. I would like to smell the fragrance of flowers that come from you, who show me so much love. [The seeds were sent by means that would ensure their arrival.]

When you look ahead, everything is dark and horrifying, but we can say, "Up to this point God has helped."

We received many letters like this and they were very encouraging, showing us that the faith of our brethren was not only unbroken, but had become more beautiful than ever.

Our suffering brethren followed the advice of the fourth-century saint Ephrem the Syrian: "When attacked, bear it; when wronged, be patient; when defamed, be forgiving; when what is yours is taken away, be thankful."

May God help us to have such attitudes!

-67-

THE STRENGTH NOT TO
BECOME DEPRESSED

*I*N ALBANIA, THE FIRST SELF-DECLARED ATHEIST State in the world, only fourteen out of 200 priests were alive when the country was liberated. Two thousand mosques and churches were destroyed. The cathedral of Tirana became a sports hall; mosques were changed into public toilets.

The results of this atheist terror? A group of 116 young couples were discovered to have gathered in Fier for the purpose of a collective marriage ceremony. The Albanian Communist press had declared that some Christians had tattooed a cross on their palm, Muslims a crescent, to make it very clear from the first handshake that they stuck to their faith in God.

In Albania, the priests Fausti and Dajani had been locked for two months in primitive latrines full of excrement. They were then condemned to death and executed. When led to the place of execution together with others, Fausti said, "Let us go to the house of the Lord." We received the following letter from the mother of the Baptist prisoner Valerii Nasaruk:

My son wished to come to the West and learn to be a preacher. God said, "No. I lead you into another school, in prison." I attended his trial. It was hard on me. I would have preferred to be in his place. But God gives one power to bear everything. The greatest trial was when they asked me in court—I his mother—to advise Valerii to change his ways. I could not do it, I comforted him. The world accuses us, his parents, for his being sentenced, saying it is the result of our teaching. Even some believers cannot understand us. But neither was our Savior understood. Even Peter warned Jesus about saving His own life. We can visit Valerii. Thank God he is courageous. He greets you all.

Valerii was courageous in prison. His mother, deprived of her son and condemned by many, through Christ had the strength not to be depressed.

-68-

LETTERS FROM
FAMILIES OF MARTYRS

*I*N RELIGIOUS LIFE, AS IN EVERY CRAFT, THERE ARE
three steps. First, one starts as a learner, a disciple.
Then one becomes a worker. Finally, if persistent,
a master. The apostle Paul calls himself a masterbuilder.

I am saddened when I meet Christians who have remained
disciples for decades, never becoming reliable workers. As for
becoming masters, able to disciple others, they do not even have
this as their aim. The Bible tells us to compete with each other
and to run so that we might get the prize, which can be obtained
only by outrunning all the others (1 Corinthians 9:24-25).

When I became a missionary, I read the history of renowned
preachers and missionaries of old and strove to attain their level
of competence and if possible to surpass it. However, I realized
that one must be prompted by a desire to serve God better, not
by personal ambition.

There are many callings in the service of the Lord, and
everyone has some gift, however modest. The calling of those of
us who work in The Voice of the Martyrs has always been to
help the persecuted Church. One privilege we have in this work
is to give support to families of martyrs. Over the years we have

received countless letters from those to whom our mission has sent help by secret channels. These have served to validate the work of our mission. I would like to share a few.

Here are excerpts from one letter:

> *Only God knows how many are in prison for their faith . . . .*
>
> *Many are expelled from their jobs for their faith . . . .*
>
> *In the churches you see thin and worn-out faces. You can see that many have come from prison . . . .*
>
> *A mother has died. The family went to the burial and they read the Holy Scriptures. But there were some spies there. These spies have lied that brethren have delivered a sermon and they were sentenced (these brethren left behind children: five for one, nine for another) . . . .*
>
> *I had to serve in the Army three years. Instead, I went to prison for five years because of the Word of God . . . . But many of the wicked people have repented and we rejoice with them in the Word of God. Then I was taken out of the concentration camp. They told us that we have filled the camp with our religion.*
>
> *There was one who could write a whole page with Bible verses. I asked him how he knew them. He answered that his beloved mother had fed him from childhood with the Word of God.*
>
> *Only God knows the sorrow which is in that house, because they have small children. They ask mother where father has gone and why he does not come back And now mother too has to leave the children to work in a collective farm.*
>
> *A young brother by the name of Vasile was on the field. They came there and bound him and took him to prison. They have taken George, too*

A mother who was left with nine children wrote:

Glory be to the Lord that He has given us also a little chip of His Cross to bear. May He only give us strength and help to bear it and to pass through the straight way reserved for Christians . . . . We must eat our bread with tears, but the Lord be praised for everything . . . .

I thank you with tears that the Lord has opened your hearts at such a big distance. May God bless and reward you for your work. May He give you a long and happy life and life eternal beyond. When we remained alone, the wicked ones said that we will not have the wherewithal to live, but praise be the Lord that He takes care, as He took care of Elijah, Daniel and of all who served Him . . . .

God has given me nine children who wait now for their father to come home, but their father put his life at stake for Christ and left his children to suffer for the faith once for all delivered by God to the saints.

From another letter from the family in which both parents died for Christ:

Know about us that we have remained orphans. May God reward your care for us and bless you with all blessings. The brethren who preached at the burial of mother were arrested. . . .

You cannot imagine how life is here. You go to bed with fear and arise with fear. The persecution is very heavy, and there are many prisoners.

Here is a letter from another family of Christian martyrs:

May the Lord Jesus who out of His free will stretched His hands on the Cross to pass us from death to life reward you with eternal life for what you sent us. I

*am content that I share the sufferings of Christ,
because if we suffer with Him, we will also rejoice
with Him . . . .A glass of water given in His name
will not be forgotten . . . .*

*A man offered 300 rubles for my New Testament.
Men are hungry for the Word of God.*

-69-

A FEW MORE
LETTERS OF COURAGE

*T*O ENCOURAGE INDIVIDUALS IN THEIR FAITH, HERE are a few more examples of those who were conquerors. When the Russian Baptist pastor, P Rumatchik, was in jail for the fifth time, he wrote these heartening words from his cell:

> *With Him, my beloved Master, it is good everywhere. With Him I have light in the dark dungeon. I had asked Him to be where I am needed, not where it is better for the outward man, but where I can bear fruit. This is my calling.*

If Church leaders speak about our relations with the Communist world, they should also question why the West should disarm before those who imprison such saints.

Another Russian Christian prisoner also wrote a moving letter:

> *I meditate here on the words of Jesus: "That whosoever believes in Him should . . . have everlasting life"*

(John 3:16). *I am among criminals. It is an under-statement that men can become like animals. Animals are without sin. But the men surrounding me in jail reach depths of devilish darkness unreachable for animals. It would be easier to live in a stable than among these criminals. Every word of theirs is filthy, every gesture repugnant. "Their throat is an open sepulchre; . . . [their] mouth is full of cursing and bitterness"* (Romans 3:13–14). *But against this background shines the love of God. Whosoever believes—even such men—can have eternal life. God sent me to prison to bring them this good news.*

In Cuba, Armando Valladares was arrested at the age of twenty-three, swiftly tried, and sentenced to thirty years in prison. He served twenty-two years of terrible torture, yet he remained a Christian. Eventually he succeeded in coming to the United States. Here he wrote how betrayed he felt by Western religious leaders who advocate disarmament instead of pleading for the Christians persecuted and tortured by the Communists. He wrote:

During those years, with the purpose of forcing us to abandon our religious beliefs and to demoralize us, the Cuban Communist indoctrinators repeatedly used the statements of support for Castro's revolution made by some representatives of Western Christian churches. Every time that a pamphlet was published in the United States, every time a clergyman would write an article in support of Fidel Castro's dictator-ship, a translation would reach us and that was worse for the Christian political prisoners than the beatings or the hunger. While we waited for the solidarity embrace from our brothers in Christ, incomprehen-sively to us, those who were embraced were our tormentors.

RICHARD WURMBRAND

To be Christian under those circumstances meant that I could not hate my tormentors. It also meant maintaining the belief that suffering was meaningful, because if man gives up his moral and religious values, or if he allows himself to be carried by a desire to hate or get revenge his existence loses all meaning. I should add that this experience has not been mine only—I saw dozens of Christians suffering and dying—committed like myself to maintaining their dignity and their richness of spirit beyond misery and pain.

Today, I remember with emotion Gerardo Gonzalez, a Protestant preacher, who knew by heart whole biblical passages and who would copy them by hand to share with his brothers in belief. I cannot forget this man whom all of us called "Brother in Faith." He interposed himself before a burst of machine-gun fire to save other prisoners who were beaten in what is known now as the massacre of Boniato prison. Gerardo repeated before dying the words said by Christ on the cross:

"Forgive them, Father, for they know not what they do. "And all of us, when the blood had dried, struggled with our consciences to attain something so difficult yet so beautiful: the ability to forgive our enemies.

In La Cabana, called the Widow-maker, Valladares lived with 350 other prisoners in a dark, humid dungeon designed to house 30 inmates. They slept in shifts on straw pallets crawling with bedbugs and lice. Flies and mosquitoes buzzed everywhere, attracted by the overflowing toilet buckets. Leeches dropped from walls, cockroaches scurried into the prisoners' rations as they ate, and hordes of rats prowled the prison, unafraid of the weakened, dying men.

Death was everywhere. The infamous El Paredon—the firing-squad wall—resounded continually. Yet Valladares prayed and wrote daily and shared his spirit of esperanza, and endured.

From a Soviet prison, Pastor M. Horev wrote:

> *I remember when my father was taken to jail. I was six. He let the police officers wait while we all knelt and prayed—the little children, mother, and then father. I remember his words: "Lord, I love my family very much. But I love You more than anything else. Therefore I choose the thorny road. I entrust my family with all its needs to You.*

I allow You to take responsibility for them. I trust that when my sufferings end I will see them before Your throne. Bless our separation. "

Horev and thousands like him entrusted their children to the heavenly Father. Where is God? He has made His home with us (John 14:23). Our homes are God's address, which means that the children of martyrs have been entrusted to us. Have we provided for these children, or have we neglected even to think about them?

In Sofia, Bulgaria, an imprisoned Christian was put in a cell the size of a man, with nails inside that pressed into his flesh at the slightest movement. When the door was locked, his first words were, "Father, forgive them, for they know not what they do." When the warden asked what this meant, he was told about the gospel. As a result, he opened the door. When the officer came, he found both prisoner and warden kneeling in adoration before God. The warden told him, "I am no longer under your orders. I belong to Christ." He too was put into prison.

Every church service should mention the martyrs and engender among believers respect for those who were willing to sacrifice all for the Christ they adored.

PART 12

MISSION TO THE MARTYRS

~70~

JUMPING OVER MOUNTAINS

I WOULD LIKE NOW TO TELL YOU ABOUT THE organization we started thirty years ago: Christian Missions to the Communist World [renamed The Voice of the Martyrs in 1992].

In spite of recent events, the Communist world is now enormous: China with its 1.1 billion inhabitants, Vietnam, Laos, Cuba, plus the considerable power Communism wields in countries that took its method of economic and political reform, and in which forty to seventy years of religious brainwashing continues to exert its influence.

Previously it included USSR, Eastern Europe, and a multitude of African states—such as Ethiopia, Somalia, Congo, Angola, Mozambique, Zimbabwe, Benin.

Thirty years ago we were a small group of people: Bishop Norderval, a Norwegian Lutheran; Stuart Harris, an English Baptist preacher; Hans Braun, a German industrialist; a Dutch pastor Maris; a Swiss lady Hedi Fluri; Hans Zarcher, a Swiss bookkeeper; Pat Henegan, owner of a South African shipping business; Colette Grossu, former prisoner of the Communists, living in France; my wife Sabina, myself, and my son Mihai and his wife Judith.

Now some might ask, "What could you few do against the immense power of Communism, as portrayed in the media?" In our planning, we did not consider it so fearsome as it was portrayed.

"But hasn't it been a world power?" Decidedly not. Communism is only one power on the ridiculously tiny earth, one of the smallest planets orbiting around a modest star, one of 100 billions in our galaxy, one of one billion galaxies. Traveling at the speed of light one can reach the sun, which is 93 million miles away, in eight minutes. To reach the edge of our galaxy would take 100,000 years at the speed of light, and it would take 10 billion years at that speed to reach what is currently the edge of the visible universe. Communism, like all earthly "isms," is a very little thing, though to us it seems like a mountain. But did not Jesus say we could move mountains—if we believed we could?

I am a Jew. In my youth I was an atheist. The words of Christ had no authority for me. Even after I accepted Him, some of His words seemed fantastic. He says, "If ye have faith as a grain of mustard seed, ye shall say unto this mountain, Remove hence to yonder place, and it shall remove" (Matthew 17:20). I tried to move mountains and did not succeed. Neither do I know any child of God who could perform such a deed.

I asked the Lord how it was that His words did not correspond to reality.

Now, a disciple of Christ should not deliver monologues in prayer, but should expect to receive answers to his questions. I received an answer to mine: "You, my beloved, cannot move mountains because your faith is not the size of a grain. You have bushels full of faith. You do not use a thousand-ton hammer, such as those employed by heavy industry, to crack open a nut. Such a hammer can only perform great works. By the same token, you are called to do greater things than amuse yourself by moving mountains. You can move God. Remember how God decided to destroy the Jewish people after they had worshiped a golden calf, and Moses through his prayer made God change His mind. To produce changes in heavenly decrees is much more important than moving mountains."

RICHARD WURMBRAND

Since then, I have stopped trying to move mountains. We are seated with Christ in heavenly places. We participate in things happening there. When in our earthly life mountains hinder us, we don't command them to move. We follow the example of Christ, about whom His bride says, "My beloved comes leaping upon the mountains, skipping upon the hills" (Song of Songs 2:8).

We need not try to remove mountains of difficulties in our own lives. We should jump over them and do our Christian duty in spite of them.

We knew the words, "He who is in you is greater than he who is in the world" (1 John 4:4). But what should we use to start a mission that we conceived of as worldwide in scope? It is written that Jesus took seven loaves that were given to Him, gave thanks, broke them, and gave them to the multitude—"They did eat, and were filled" (Mark 8:8). Suppose the disciples had not seven but only three loaves or only one. What would have happened? The multitude would have been satisfied just the same. As a matter of fact, on another occasion Jesus used only five loaves instead of seven, fed an even bigger multitude, and a greater number of baskets full of fragments remained behind (Mark 8:19–20).

We realized we could serve God with the very little we had. His blessings do not depend upon the size or quantity of what we have but upon the fact that we bring them to Him.

But suppose we have nothing to bring—what then? But that is impossible—the Hebrew, Aramean, and Greek languages in which the Bible was written did not have the word "zero" or its mathematical symbol " V " A person who has nothing to bring to Jesus does not exist.

We can bring ourselves, even if we have to honestly say, "I possess nothing." We have something very valuable: ourselves and our utter poverty. We can bring our sins to Jesus. From the sin of being a fanatical persecutor, God made Saul of Tarsus a zealous apostle. From the sin of a loose life, Jesus made Mary Magdalene a saint with steadfast love. If we bring our weakness to Christ, which we surely have, His strength will show its perfection in our weakness.

Our mission began with very little—almost nothing, in fact. But instead of using this little directly, we brought it to Jesus. He multiplied it and greatly blessed it.

—71—

By All Means

E DECIDED TO SPREAD THE GOSPEL IN Communist countries. By what means? Only one is biblical. Paul writes that it was his purpose to save souls "by all means" (1 Corinthians 9:22). He who is choosy about the means of propagating the gospel is not biblical.

While we respected Communist laws, we interpreted them in our own manner or broke them. To give just a few examples, we threw thousands of plastic bags into the Bering Straits separating Alaska from the USSR, into the Black Sea near the shores of the Ukraine, and into the sea between the Greek islands and Albania. Each tightly sealed bag contained the Gospel in the local language or a brochure showing the way of salvation, and a piece of chewing gum to induce even the worst Communist policeman to open the bag. We also enclosed pieces of straw to make the bag float on the water. Waves brought the bags to shore. We had studied the currents in the sea to be sure they would arrive as we planned. The method worked.

When Albania opened up for religion recently, we met a man who had found such a Gospel, was converted through reading it, and from then on watched the shore to find others, which he distributed. Discovered, he spent nine years in jail for this "crime."

We asked him, "Are you angry at us? If it weren't for our activity, you wouldn't have been in prison."

He replied, "It was worth it."

After nine years in jail for Christ, he was able for the first time to attend church, and he received a Bible.

We also flew the message of Christ in balloons from West to East Germany, from South to North Korea. People are saved by all mean—even by poor means. The Albanian did not require a whole Bible, much less volumes of theology. He was saved by only one Gospel message, which sustained him for nine years as a prisoner of Christ.

As we grew, we smuggled in Bibles and Christian literature by land, by sea, by tourists, by diplomats, by any means we could devise. We also smuggled in printing presses piece by piece, which were then assembled and sometimes put to work literally underground. The work entailed tremendous risks, but the rewards outweighed them by far. We created bookstores, print shops, mission centers in Romania, Hungary, Russia, Ethiopia, China. We were relentless in our endeavors.

72

Unfounded Hopes
Are Founded

ROM PRISON, I HAD WRITTEN TO MY FAMILY, "THE most unfounded hope is much more founded than the most founded despair." At that point I had been sentenced to twenty years of forced labor and was deathly ill. I hoped then that once I was free and capable of working I would be able to help other persecuted children of God and spread the gospel to Communist countries far and wide. In my case, this hope came true. For twenty-five years I have been in the free world, and God has used me to create an international mission that has fulfilled my dream.

My family and I came to the West as poor, unknown immigrants, our only treasure our vision and our unfounded hope. We had no means to fulfill it. But despair is useless. Hope is a force to be reckoned with.

During these years there have been threats against my life, including the constant danger of being kidnapped. Sometimes simple swindlers, at other times Church leaders, who perhaps did not realize they served the Communist cause instead of God's, attacked us. But I nurtured only hope. In all our adversities God made us more than conquerors. Thousands of believers on earth and angels in heaven made our earnest dream, as are all dreams that come from God, a reality.

At a wedding in Cana, Jesus was told, "Every man at the beginning does set forth good wine; and when men have well drunk, then that which is worse. But thou hast kept the good wine until now" (John 2: 10). The devil sometimes gives good things first: beautiful promises, selfish pleasures. After one has drunk deeply, a worse wine follows: wrecked lives, remorse, spiritual blindness—and in the end, the worst, eternal damnation.

Love knows that the best things are yet to come. Now it tastes the joy of obeying God's commands and delights in the fellowship of Christ, His holy angels, and the great communion of saints. This joy is for the present mingled with the bitterness of the cross. Now it is a glory in tribulations, distress, persecution, and nakedness. But in the midst of tears and the shedding of blood, the bride of Christ never ceases to hope. She knows her Bridegroom has stored up in His banqueting house the best of wines for the future. She is not in a hurry. Loves does not hasten to obtain results. She can bear with transitory failures, sufferings and defeats. The ultimate victory is hers.

We had nothing to fear. In September 1970, I wrote to all our missions:

> The church of Christ is not endangered by Communism. Even the gates of hell cannot prevail against her. It is Communism that is endangered by the existence of the Church, because the final victory is ours. We have won for Christ the daughter of Stalin, the greatest mass-murderer of Christians; Mrs Kosygin, the wife of the Russian dictator; Pasternak Solzhenitsyn, Siniavski, and other first-rank Soviet writers, formerly members of the Communist Party. We don't tremble before Communism. It should be in a panic because of us. The best of wines are stored up for the children of God.

There were a few little victories that the persecuted Church had won by then. It continued to survive on hope, as did we. We fervently believed our teaching was correct: "Hate Communism, but love the Communists. Break through the Iron Curtain with the gospel and the prayers of saints." Communist governments have fallen. The Word of God is now disseminated freely in many countries of the former Communist bloc, whereas only a short time ago it was a crime to own or share a Bible. We helped the churches in Communist countries not only with Bibles, but also with Christian literature, radio, printing facilities, and material aid. In all these things we also gave them something else—we gave them our love.

There has always been persecution of religion, as well as heroism. But under Fascism and Communism, mankind saw its spiritual midnight—and God's people their spiritual zenith. Today in many parts of the world there are still atrocities against those of other beliefs, but nowhere else have they been practiced on such a large scale as they were in the USSR.

Blessings at Midnight

The earth turns on its axis. Midnight is the moment when a part of the earth is the farthest away from the sun. Spiritual midnight is the period of the greatest departure of men from God. Today our generation has experienced unmentionable events in a midnight of unparalleled darkness. But midnight is not received with the same feelings by the children of God as by the world. At midnight, the firstborn of the Egyptians died, but the chosen people obtained their freedom.

The Lord said, "The night comes when no man can work" (John 9:4). But whenever something is declared impossible in the Bible, this does not refer to the faithful. About them Jesus declared, "All things are possible to him that believes" (Mark 9:23).

God's people can work even at midnight. It was at midnight that Samson took the gates of the city of Gaza (Judges 16:3). At midnight, Ruth received from Boaz the promise, "I will do to you all that you require" (Ruth 3:811). At midnight, Paul and Silas won for the Lord the jailer of Philippi (Acts 16:25). At midnight, the people of God do their greatest exploits. Therefore, the psalmist says, "At midnight I will rise to give thanks unto thee" (Psalm 119:62).

Christians must not be afraid of the darkness in the world. They must work. The Bridegroom comes soon. True children of God cannot meet Him emptyhanded.

~73~

Two Opposing Attitudes

HE COMMUNISTS KNOW THIS BETTER THAN WE DO. At one point the Hungarian government allowed religious instruction in schools, but on one condition: the saints and martyrs of all times were not to be mentioned. They understand all too well what effect their lives would have on students. A church that does not teach the example of saints is purposeless and surely harmless, as far as the atheists are concerned.

Therefore our mission has done just the opposite. During a session of the Anglican Synod in London, Canon Stephens paid us a great compliment: "Wurmbrand provided the church with a dimension which was necessary . . . a great moving sense of the presence of Christ in the modern confessors and martyrs."

"Absence of martyrs and saints in religious teaching" is a commandment of the Communists that is also respected by innumerable Western churches. But our mission has pointed to the example of martyrs in order to open hearts to the communion of angels and Christ. This is the proper teaching.

When Georgi Vins was first sentenced to five years in jail and five years of deportation, he addressed the prosecutor and judges at his trial as follows:

I don't see in you enemies. You are my brothers and sisters in the great human family. After I have left the courthouse, I will pray in my cell to God for you all, that He may reveal to you His divine truth and the marvelous sense of life. It is the Bible which formed me. It is the Bible which has taught me always to tell the truth.

It is significant that Vins understood the importance of learning from martyrs. His book, *The Family Chronicle*, originally smuggled out of Russia, was nothing more than a series of lives of martyrs, beginning with his own parents and relatives. This is how a real Christian leader writes Church history.

Read again his words of love toward his persecutors, who destroyed his parents and himself in jails. Look with the same love upon your enemies. Then you will begin to realize that they have guardian angels, too, and you will have opened your heart to the unseen world.

Five hundred years ago, Girolamo Savonarola said:

Death is the most solemn moment of our life. Then it is that the evil one makes his last attack on us. It is as though he were always playing chess with man, and awaiting the approach of death to give checkmate. He who wins at that moment wins the battle of life. [Savonarola was a Dominican friar who was excommunicated and executed in 1498 for criticizing Pope Alexander VI.]

We lead you to the bare boards on which a Christian martyr dies and conquers. We urge you to become this kind of follower of Christ.

74

STEALING FROM GOD

COMMUNIST OFFICER WHO CAME TO ARREST a pastor asked him, "Do you consider me a monster, as everyone else does?"

The pastor, repressing any natural revulsion toward his oppressor, loved the man and answered: "Monster? No, I see an unhappy man who believes that no one loves him. But God loves you, and in a special way. It was for evil men that He became man. He did not come to earth because we were nice altar-boys, but because we were dirty. The dirtier we are, the more right we have to His pity."

The officer defended himself. "I am not as bad as that. I am not a thief."

"You are," answered the pastor. "You have stolen from God."

"What?" came the sharp retort. "How?"

"You have robbed Him of your sins. Our sins belong to Him. To take them as His property, He came to be born as the Son of man. The dirt of our evil deeds are His, not yours. If you refuse to give them to Him, the Lamb of God who takes away the sin of the world, who has the right to take them away because they are His property, you are a thief. Only a robber keeps what belongs to someone else."

That night the pastor remained unimprisoned.

In our day, Communism is the greatest sin committed by mankind. It robs Jesus of what belongs to Him: the sins of all of us. In our fight against the evils of this ideology, we realize we are dealing not with some human weakness but with tremendous devilish forces that control the actions of men.

Jesus equated sin with sickness (Matthew 9:11-12). Communists have a disgusting, contagious sickness. Devils rule them, therefore we must love them. But all the while we must hate their sickness. Communism is powerful, but the Savior has given us even greater power to cast out these devils and heal people of the deadly disease of Communism, and of compromise with Communism.

We as Christians are unworthy to lift our eyes to God, but our vocation can be touched by no one. It pleased God to call such sinners as you and me to heal sickness and to cast out devils. At The Voice of the Martyrs we engage in this fight undaunted by our own frailty because we do so in His strength.

-75-

THE MADNESS OF MEN

*J*ESUS MUST HAVE PONDERED MUCH ABOUT THE madness of men. While carrying His cross to Golgotha, He quoted the words of Hosea: "They shall say to the mountains, 'Cover us!' and to the hills, 'Fall on us!'" (Hosea 10:8). Only madmen can speak thus, instead of saying, "Let us pray to God that He will protect us," or "Let us seek shelter." What good does it do to have a mountain fall on you?

What would Jesus say about today's madness?

In the nineteenth century, missionaries went to give the gospel to African cannibals. Some missionaries were eaten. When Bishop Hannington was devoured in Uganda, his two sons went to replace him. Eventually they baptized and gave communion to men who had digested their own father's flesh. These men told the sons that the bishop, while being led to his death, repeated unceasingly Jesus' words, "Love your enemies."

Modern men are worse than cannibals, who, with practical intent, kill men in order to eat them. We do not eat humans, so why did we kill tens of millions in world wars, why did Fascists and Communists kill more tens of millions in the years before and after?

It is folly to ask why men kill. They are mad and must be brought to the fear of God.

Corrie ten Boom related how Christians in Nazi death camps discussed ways to bring Nazis to salvation. God used me to form a mission to Communists, radical Muslims, terrorists—men worse than cannibals. Why doesn't the world church declare this as its purpose? Why have there been so many Christian congresses without a word on the subject of winning to Christ the members of Communist parties and youth organizations?

The explanation is that many of us have not become really God-fearing, that many Christians still share the madness of the world. I wish every reader were a Christian, but not an average one. We should be serious in our thinking.

RICHARD WURMBRAND

~76~

CHRISTIANS INFILTRATED
THE SECRET POLICE

*I*N THE SIXTIES, THE NAME OF NIKOLAI KOKHLOV appeared in a BBC documentary. A captain of the Soviet Secret Police, he was given the assignment of going to West Germany to infiltrate the Russian Freedom Movement and assassinate its leader, Dr. Okolovitch. He simply had to open a box of cigarettes concealing a silent gun firing cyanide bullets and Dr. Okolovitch would have been finished.

The infiltrator was received into the Liberation movement and was invited to the flat of its leader. But instead of killing him, Kokhlov put the murder weapon on the table and told his story. He and his wife were underground Christians who had infiltrated the Communist Secret Police. His wife had warned him, "If you kill, I shall divorce you." He had no need of this injunction, since he believed in Christ wholeheartedly. He had fulfilled his duty of love and saved the life of a man condemned to death by the Communists. Then the Communists tried to poison their supposed agent, putting a deadly dose of thallium in his coffee in a restaurant in West Germany. They did not succeed.

Many people like Kokhlov became Christians through a Bible or other Christian book smuggled into Russia by some mission. We believe that much of it was due to the work of our organization because out of all mission organizations claiming to work behind the Iron Curtain, ours seemed to have a monopoly on being constantly attacked by the Communist press. Obviously, the Communist attacked those Christian organizations that were harming them the most.

One such brutal attack that mentioned our name on four pages appeared in the Soviet periodical Znanie in January of 1974. Shortly after, another appeared in the Soviet newspaper Radianska Ukraina, which contained a gruesome story about the killing of tens of thousands of Jews, Ukrainians, and Poles during the war and about other killings during the Russian Revolution. These mass murders were not perpetrated by counter-revolutionists or Nazis, claim the Soviets, but by Evangelicals and Baptists. Because they were not successful in overthrowing the Soviet regime, the newspaper said, these Christians, who are in reality Fascists, tried to kill the souls of the Soviet population by smuggling Bibles. The leaders of this "criminal activity" were Pastor Richard Wurmbrand and the director of the Swedish Slavic mission, Brother Martinson.

～77～

TRANSPARENT PURITY

*W*HEN THE JEW AVRAM SHIFFIN WAS IN A Soviet jail for his Zionist activities, he met a 72-year-old Baptist named Solodiankin, about whom he wrote the following:

The goodness and transparent purity of that man made a huge impression. Even the soldiers who guarded us became better when he was there. Everything he earned as a slave laborer he used like this: half for his sick daughter and 25% for his church. From the rest (7 or 8 rubles) he bought for himself a little sugar and bread; the rest he gave to the sick prisoners in the camp.

Solodiankin was almost blind, and his glasses had been broken by the interrogator. Shiffin told him that he had a Bible and was ready to read it to him. In the evening, Solodiankin came. He had changed his shirt and combed his hair with great care. "To read the eternal book is a feast," he said.

The Jew read to the Christian from Isaiah. At a certain moment, he was interrupted: "You made a mistake."

It was true. "But do you know the text by heart?"

"Of course," replied Solodiankin.

"Then why should I read it to you?" Shiffin asked.

"Because it is a joy for me to hear the Scriptures. One gets new ideas."

Once when the prisoners were compelled to listen to a lecture about Lenin, Solodiankin arose and contradicted the speaker publicly: "Why do you make a god out of a simple man? Throughout history many have been honored like him as big men, but what are they before the Creator?" For this he was punished.

During that time we were smuggling Bibles into the USSR. Some who claimed smuggling was wrong reproached us roundly. But without smuggling, blind Solodiankin and thousands like him would have remained without the Word of God.

We praise God for such men as Solodiankin and Jews who read the Bible to them. We adore God who does these great works, and we will continue to smuggle Christian books wherever barriers exist (certain Christian literature and Bibles are still forbidden in China, Vietnam, and many Muslim countries).

78

GOD'S SMUGGLING WORK

*S*OME CRITICS HAVE ADVISED US OVER THE YEARS, though in vain, to stop smuggling Christian literature because smuggling is immoral. If smuggling is immoral, why does God engage in the practice?

Let's look back at the story of Jesus. The Jewish high priests had a promise from God that He would speak to them from between the two cherubim on the ark of the covenant in the Temple. They felt safe. Never would the Messiah dare to come without telling them in advance. No ruler from abroad would visit a country without giving notice. Thus the Roman governor was also sure. The King of the Jews could not appear in the world without his knowledge.

One night, the Light of the world "smuggled" himself into Palestine as a baby, after having been in the womb of a holy virgin, contrary to accepted moral standards and the laws of biology. What a pity that the critics of Bible smuggling did not live at that time! They would have had something against which to protest.

Some Soviet church leaders, knowing that if arrested they might be tortured to death, went into hiding, which is possible only by assuming a false identity. "Deceit!" some cry. "Lack of integrity!" But God lived on earth without telling people who He was. The people of Nazareth thought they were dealing with a carpenter bearing the common Jewish name "Jeshua." Later, when some began to believe He was the Messiah, He entreated them not to tell anyone, exactly as an underground worker under Communism or Islam would do.

Then Jesus was crucified and buried. A seal was put on His grave by the authorities. Now everyone knows that one is not supposed to break a seal. But angels are not bound by earthly laws. An angel just rolled away the stone, without worrying about the seal.

Would today's Christian magazines have advised Jesus to abide by the law and remain in the tomb after the authorities had sealed it? But Jesus "smuggled" himself out of the grave into life again. Some tell us that we should not break the laws of Communist tyrants. Jesus "broke" the law of gravity and ascended into heaven!

What do these critics really know about love for the Word of God and for the Church? In some cases, Christians in the Soviet Union did not fret when a church was locked and sealed by the authorities. They cautiously unlocked it with another key so as not to damage the seal in its place.

We continue to denounce the crimes of the Communists and Islam and to smuggle Christian literature into the Communist and Muslim camp, telling people about the resurrected Savior who makes possible our resurrection.

We asked a Russian brother who collaborated with us in this secret work if his conscience did not tell him to be submissive to the authorities. His answer amazed us:

> If we are wrong, the whole Baptist religion is wrong. I read an article in our secret magazine that told about Thomas Helwys, pastor of the first Baptist church on English soil. He went to prison because he had said that the king had no power over the immortal souls of his subjects, to make laws and ordinances for them and to put spiritual rulers over them.

I read about a letter smuggled out of prison in England in 1620 by a Baptist, John. The letter was written in milk just as we do now so the jailers would not notice. Our families knew how to make the letters readable. John wrote, "The magistrate can only compel the body, not the mind and the conscience."

If we are wrong, John Bunyan was a fool! He preferred to sit twelve years in prison rather than worship in a manner determined by someone else. And for him it was only a matter of complying with another form of Christian religion, whereas we have had to comply with regulations imposed by atheists.

Some feared and went back to the official church under pressure. But they were an infinitesimal minority. The Underground Church continued. The Christian people stood with us.

Even some Communists and police officers rendered us a precious service.

Men saved in the highest sense of the word are also saved from codes of conduct purportedly established once and forever for all circumstances. They have the Holy Spirit to give them personal guidance in extraordinary situations.

From a subterranean prison in Rome, St. Paul wrote, "I can do all things through Christ who strengthens me" (Philippians 4:13). He was not, however, tortured as Communists have tortured Christians in our day.

In Red China's prisons, some of our brethren and sisters in the faith had to sit motionless, leaning toward the wall, from five in the morning until nine o'clock at night, day after day, month after month, for years. Every day was like an enemy determined to torture them to death. They were not allowed to speak to the other inmates of the cell and were forbidden either to laugh or to weep. If a prisoner had to cough, he had to say to the warden who continually spied on him, "Bau-gau", which means "Please give me permission." It was "Bau-gau" for spitting, for scratching oneself, for killing vermin, for using the toilet.

If all at once someone in the cell went mad and began to sing, the rest had to sit motionless while their fellow-prisoner was silenced through beatings. With chains on their hands and feet, they could not even help him.

In Hebrews 13:3, it is written, "Remember them that are in bonds, as bound with them." Try to sit for as little as six hours like this, motionless, on the floor (in prison, on the cold concrete) to see how your brethren fare!

RICHARD WURMBRAND

-79-

MARTYRS OF OUR MISSION

THE DICTATOR IDI AMIN KILLED BROTHER JOSEPH Kiwanuka, trustee of our mission in Uganda. Amin had falsely accused him of belonging to the CIA, only because he distributed our literature.

At that time, Amin was the only ruler who received arms from the Soviet Union as a gift, so he obeyed his benefactors. In his eyes, everyone who denounced the crimes of Communism, showing the better way of Christ, was an agent of "American imperialism."

Brother Kiwanuka received a warning and fled to neighboring Kenya. The Ugandan police kidnapped him out of a flying helicopter. His crushed body was drowned in Lake Victoria. He left behind a widow and many children. In addition, the whole Christian tribe of Lugbanas was killed by Amin.

Wang-Shin-Mei was beaten to death while on assignment to smuggle Christian literature into Red China for us. Another man involved in our courier work disappeared somewhere in Cuba. The translator of my book, Tortured for Christ, in Amharic, Ethiopia, was put into jail. To make this book known was considered a crime by the Communists. Today he still suffers from the mistreatment he endured. Now he leads our mission center in Addis Ababa. His name is Testsray Neffrim.

The Burmese pastor Wy-Foo died by being hanged head down in China. He had been caught smuggling our literature over the frontier.

Your life might be smooth if you decide to walk with Jesus all the way, but it might also be very tempestuous at times. The reward is that if Jesus lives within you, you will be an overcomer and will sit with Him on His throne.

~80~

PERSON ATTACKS

I HAVE TO WARN YOU THAT THE DISCIPLE CANNOT be above his master. Jesus was attacked personally with insults and slander. If you walk the road toward masterdom, you can expect the same treatment.

The apostle Paul's main subject in his epistles was the One whose countenance shines like the sun releasing its splendor, whose eyes are pure, and whose whole being is as snowy as white jade. Christ is the main subject—but not the only one. Sometimes Paul wrote about himself and his co-workers. So you will forgive us if we give ourselves as examples in this matter.

Over the years our mission specifically, and I personally, have been the targets of fierce criticism and vilification on the part of the Communists and their stooges. The Soviet Union sent a protest to the French government for allowing Solzhenitsyn to speak on television. The Swiss authorities informed our mission that they received a similar protest against the advertisements announcing my books. In Finland, where the film of Solzhenitsyn's novel, One Day in the Life of Ivan Denisovich, was forbidden, the government, acting under Soviet pressure, asked the Lutheran bishops not to grant me the use of churches. As a result, I had to preach in privatelyowned halls.

The Communists forced the owners of the hall in Helsinki to cancel the agreement. The administrator of a hall in Turku belonging to the fire brigade replied to the Communists, "When a fire breaks out, our boys go to quench it, risking their lives without asking to what party the man belongs whose house is burning. The cry of every suffering person can be shouted in this hall. Wurmbrand brings the cries of martyrs. He will speak here." She had more courage than the Lutheran bishops.

A book published in Russia, *Diversion Without Dynamite*, by Belov and Shilkin, concentrated heavily on our international organization, on me and my son. It described our activities as "tempestuous." The story told about me was that I was allegedly sentenced in Romania for anti-Communist activity under the guise of religion. Then the authors claimed that all our assertions about persecution in the Soviets were fanciful. What hurt them most was my book, *Was Marx a Satanist?* (now titled *Marx and Satan*), which has been translated and continually reprinted in many languages. "Wurmbrand is among the most ardent opponents of detente"—the authors even praised anti-Communists if they have the one virtue of also being anti-Wurmbrand.

In an article in Nauka i Religia, principal atheist magazine of Moscow, these same authors said that "Wurmbrand's temperament might be envied by the greatest football players. His shouting is savage. This fighter calls for a crusade against Socialism, which he calls an offspring of Satan. He was imprisoned in Romania for distributing religious literature inciting against the government." In this article, two things were remarkable. First, that I was called a "devilish pastor" for my book on Marx, though the authors produced not one single fact to refute the documentation of my thesis. Second, the article congratulated Christian leaders, even anti-Communists, who took a stand against me. They might be adversaries of Communism, but as long as they opposed me, one of the chief enemies of Communism, they were approved by Moscow.

In view of the foregoing, we are not surprised about attacks against us in the West. These attacks have occurred in many countries. For instance, an Italian paper lambasted our Italian director, Dr. Laiso, for his anti-Communist speeches over our radio station in Marchirolo, calling them "infamies." It is "infamy" in their view to say that Communists have killed and continue to kill millions of innocents and that they aim at abolishing all religion.

In a book entitled, *Soviet Evangelicals*, a Mr. Savatsky attacked us as follows:

> *The Wurmbrand mission fits the image of 19th century mission imperialism. It is anti-Communist. It is as much committed to the overthrow of Communism as to helping believers in Communist societies. In Wurmbrand's world view, a Christian must oppose Communism, which logically means Soviet Christians must be anti-Communist, perhaps also unpatriotic. The Wurmbrand position confirms the charges of Soviet writers that religion is the servant of reactionary capitalism. In Wurmbrand's view, genuine Christians in the USSR can be only those who are suffering. Those who are not apparently suffering, as the official Baptist leadership, must obviously be tools of the political police.*
>
> *Wurmbrand insists that in a battle situation one can have only friends and enemies, and therefore one plays into the enemy's hands if one acknowledges complex nuances, draws attention to gray areas. Wurmbrand's writings are predominant in the religious bookstores of America and Europe, which means the majority of concerned Christians have formed their image of Christians in the USSR through his influence and distortions.*

Then follows the greatest compliment of all: "Through these missions large numbers of Bibles and other Christian literature have become available in the Soviet Union, and the Bible hunger has eased noticeably."

This admission we cherished!

Doubtless you have never heard of Klaus Kempner, but at one time he wore the imposing title of Supreme National Counselor of the Lutheran Church in West Germany. He circulated behind our back a letter indicating that he had spent three years studying "the problem of Wurmbrand." Now the devil tries hard to trick me into pride. To be the object of study of a Supreme Counselor for three years could mean something. This study was so important that the Counselor forgot to warn his parishioners about the Communist danger and never told them about the martyrs of today After three years, he found out that I put much sentiment into my messages. The Counselor considered this a mistake. But should sermons be dry and boring? He accuses me also of being a mystic. This Supreme Lutheran Counselor does not know that Luther took his teaching from the mystic, Tauler.

Another accusation: "Wurmbrand paints only with black and white and knows with absolute surety who are the children of light and the children of darkness." I accept this accusation. The Communist torturers and those who cover up their crimes are darker than the night; those who give their lives for Christ in Communist prisons and those who help them are whiter than snow. So we think.

The Supreme Counselor did not approve of my followers. He emphasized that they were mostly men of personal piety, without academic degrees. He, the Counselor, forgot that the apostles were such men. He also said that it was not good to call Wurmbrand a deceiver or a psychopath, since these things have always been said about the prophets, so he called me the creator of a new sect. He went on to say that in my view salvation depends not on faith in Jesus Christ but upon my own message. These accusations were patently ridiculous. The Lutheran church of West Germany, as well as other churches, should have been helping families of Christian martyrs with a piece of bread and fighting Communism in their own country, instead of trying to feed my pride.

RICHARD WURMBRAND

The principal slander against us is that we engage in politics, not religion.

Christians should not get involved in cheap politics, but they should join in the battle to free the whole world from the rule of Satan, because it is commanded by Jesus, though it is unpopular and might lead to loss of life. Jesus praised a good Samaritan who helped a man wounded by robbers. Suppose the Samaritan had come that way half an hour earlier, while the robbers were beating the victim? Would he have said, "I am a pacifist. I don't mix in violent fights. Finish beating him up, and then I will pour wine and oil on his wounds"? Or would he have organized a protest march against the beating, announcing to the robbers that the police force had been withdrawn? Or would love have prompted him to fight in defense of the innocent?

We know the answer. Divine love would not have allowed the good Samaritan to stand aside, and the commandment to us is: imitate him. Whoever keeps this commandment will be loved by Christ. It is the government's calling to lead the fight on the diplomatic, military, cultural, and economic fields. As a religious organization we lead only a spiritual fight. This has to be consistent, without the slightest compromise, like our personal fight against sin. We belong to a heroic God.

The best thing is to concur with your slanderer and help him spread his slander. Although not everything he says about you might be true, basically he is right in describing you as a sinner. He helps you by destroying your pride and depriving you of glory which is due only to God. So you will not mind false accusations, let alone true, against you. They will not hurt you a bit if you fulfill the first command of Jesus: "If anyone desires to come after me, let him deny himself" (Matthew 16:24).

Christians can listen quietly to all evil spoken about them. They are not the ones attacked. They have abandoned the old personalities and have identified with Jesus. I myself have the worst opinion about everything in Wurmbrand that is a remnant of the old, which is not from Jesus.

~*81*~

REMEMBER THOSE WHO SUFFER

*S*OME WONDER WHY THE CHURCHES HAVEN'T cared about the multitude of Christians persecuted in Communist countries. This kind of neglect has a long history.

St. Paul wrote, "No church communicated with me as concerning giving and receiving" (Philippians 4:15). He had founded many churches himself, but when he, and probably many others, entered prison for the faith, his brethren did not realize that prison means hunger, destitution, anguish of soul. They did not realize that prisons also have much to give to the Church. For Christian prisoners, the fact that Jesus enters through locked doors bringing peace is not simply an old Easter story. It happens every day in their cells. Their experiences can enrich the followers of Christ. Christians did not sense that the suffering of some is a rich treasure from which all can draw that hands wearing chains can bless well. So it happened that no church had communicated with Paul when he was a prisoner, concerning giving and receiving, except the Philippians.

There exists an invincible indifference, insensitivity, and apathy toward suffering. We sometimes wonder why people do not react when they are told the story of the Cross of Christ, why they remain unmoved when they hear about the sufferings of Christians in Communist countries.

There was a multitude on Golgotha who attended the crucifixion of men and who actually heard their cries when nails were hammered into their hands and feet. They must have known that at least One of them was the best of men. Otherwise He would not have prayed for His torturers or cared to bring a robber to God, while passing through unspeakable physical suffering himself. Now this Jesus cried, as in despair, "My God, my God, why hast thou forsaken me?" And what was the reaction of the multitude? They said to each other, "Let be, let us see . . . " It did not pass through their minds to alleviate His suffering by at least giving Him a little bit of water or a word of compassion. "Let be, let us see whether Elias will come to save Him" (Matthew 27:49).

Elias [Elijah] is not only the proper name of a prophet of old. It is in Hebrew a short sentence which means, "Jehovah is my God." In this sense everyone can be an Elias. In this sense the Lord said that St. John the Baptist was Elias. Each of us must have Jehovah as our God. If the compassionate God Jehovah is master of our life, we will never remain impassive when we see innocent suffering.

Those who are in reality without God have this attitude, "Let be, let us see." People of this type attended the crucifixion on Golgotha and were not moved by it. Those same type of people today are not moved by the message of the Underground Church. They do not care if the little brethren of Jesus are hungry or in jail. They will answer at the judgment for their indifference and neglect. We pity them.

There exists an even worse category.

The Gadarenes began to pray Jesus "to depart out of their coasts" (Mark 5:17). They had good reason to do so. Jesus had chased demons out of a man by ordering them to enter into a herd of swine, which then ran down a slope straight into the sea and drowned. The Gadarenes thus lost their whole property— the bread for themselves and their children. It meant nothing to them that the man had been cured.

How would you react if the entrance of Jesus into your life meant the loss of your house, car, bank account, and job? You might perhaps continue to use holy phrases without meaning them. The Gadarenes uttered a prayer that was at least sincere: "Depart from us, Jesus."

Jesus is used to being driven out. When Holman Hunt painted his renowned picture "The Light of the World," in which the Lord is shown seeking entrance, knocking at the door of a house, His feet are turned not toward the door but the roadway. He has more chance to be refused than accepted, because to accept Him costs much.

The apostle Paul writes, "For Christ Jesus my Lord, I have suffered the loss of all things and do count them but dung, that I may win Christ" (Philippians 3:8). Do we also look upon our nice furniture, a new car, the better job we just got, the money we possess, as upon repulsive dung? When someone encounters dung, they wish to get away from it—the sooner the better. Is this our attitude toward earthly possessions? Whoever wishes to win Christ must lose their attachment to them.

Friendship with Jesus is costly. Faith alone saves, but saving faith is never alone. It is always accompanied by great sacrifices for Christ's sake.

As we bring sacrifices to Him, let us have full understanding for those who do not have the power to offer them, who remain indifferent to our sufferings or even increase them.

81

FROM THE EXPERIENCES
OF OUR MISSIONS

*J*ESUS SAID, "IF THINE EYE OFFEND THEE, PLUCK IT out" (Mark 9:47). The Aramaean language that Jesus spoke was extremely poor. It did not have the words "idea, sentiment, passion, intention, intuition, perspective, manner of looking at things." For all these different notions Jesus had to use the word "eye." He never intended that we should pluck out our physical eye, which never offends. Plucking it out would not be helpful, since blind men commit as many sins as those who see.

But he taught us to pluck out decidedly from our mind a certain manner of looking at reality. We have a lacrimal system [tear glands] given by God, and we are meant to use it rightly. "Weep with those who weep," wrote Paul (Romans 12:15). Jesus wept when He saw His friends Mary and Martha in grief. Don't use your tears so much for your own sorrows! What you think about the events of your life may be wrong.

The tears of two women were floating side by side down the Mississippi River. The first tear said, "I am the tear of a woman who lost her lover." The second tear replied, "And I am the tear of the woman who got him."

Shed tears for the sufferings of others, thus showing them your love and sympathy. It is only with tears in your eyes that you can see reality clearly. Weep with God's weeping about the sins of the world, including your own.

When our political leadership discussed the relative merits of various weapons systems, we advocated the love bomb and the gospel missile. Mao said rightly, "It is not important what weapons the enemy has, but rather what the man who uses the weapons thinks." We felt that the Soviet Union should be "attacked" on a large front with the gospel, with the teaching of love. Every converted Soviet citizen would then be a sympathizer of the West, where Christianity is free, and a foe of the satanic system oppressing him. The Church is separate from the state in most countries of the free world. This is an arrangement benefitting the inner life of a nation, but the gospel can be a powerful weapon for winning a large population of an inimical country to our side. Then the terrible option of killer weapons systems will be avoided.

There are always Christians who say, "We should just preach the gospel and not bother about Communism or democracy." They have expressed their disagreement with my anti-Communism. "Christianity can live in every form of society," they claim.

I wonder where they learned their gospel.

Did Livingstone know the gospel? When he went to Africa, there existed a booming slave trade. According to the theology of my critics, he should have allowed the slaves to remain slaves and not have preached to them about Christ. He had read in the Bible about how God freed the Jewish slaves. He could not remain unmoved when he saw the gangs of slaves, bound at the wrist to a long chain, beaten with whips, exactly like prisoners of the Communists in Red China and the Soviet Union as they were being transported.

"These terrible things made Dr. Livingstone burn with anger," wrote Maskey Miller in his *History of South Africa*. Many Christians today have lost the virtue of becoming angry about slavery. Some never get angry except at a Wurmbrand and our missions, which have always fought against Communist slavery. Livingstone never forgot to beg the British people to put down the terrible trade in human flesh and blood. He succeeded. Slavery was abolished in the British empire—only to be reintroduced in our day by Communist African governments.

Today Livingstone's body lies in Westminster Abbey, while those in our churches who claim to honor his memory criticize us for opposing a form of slavery that has engulfed whole nations. The gospel we preach includes the mandate, "Let my people go!"

From our first beginnings over thirty years ago, we always aimed to create a spirit of concern for the persecuted, to stimulate prayer for them everywhere, and to encourage Christians in many lands to supply Bibles and literature for areas where they were forbidden. Other similar organizations acknowledged their indebtedness to us. As a result, millions have been reached by our work in Communist countries and the free world.

It began with very few who remembered the words of John Chrysostom:

> *The power of the righteous consists not in their number but in the grace of the Spirit. There were twelve apostles. How little leaven! All men were unbelievers. How much the dough! But those twelve turned the world upside down. Let only ten change, and soon they will be twenty, the twenty will become 100, the 100 will become 1,000, and the 1,000, a whole town.*
>
> *Just as the lighting of ten candles can give light to a whole house, so it is with spiritual acts. Let only ten change and we can start afire that will give light to all.*

To do this we needed sanctification. We had to strive hard for this. The Greek word for sanctification is *haghiasmos*, which means to become unearthly (*ha*, not, and *gheos*, earthly). We were human and had our temptations. We could not fight Communism outwardly without fighting inwardly as well.

Sexual impulses are very strong. They have defeated many Christians, but we fought to subdue them. There have been falling into sin, but also rising from sin to even greater purity. We had to be honest in money matters and strive to attain the other virtues as well. Yet sanctification comprehends more than this. It means accepting lovingly any cross given by God. It means putting Christ above any earthly attachment, even our own families and our own lives.

We sing easily, "Let goods and kindred go, this mortal life also." We had to do more than sing. We had to let them go. We had great examples before us.

The Russian monk Amphilochia, while in prison, had cold water poured on his naked body in freezing weather. Another, Gregor, had been tortured to death. His fingers had been cut off and his back flayed in the sign of the cross.

Macarius knew something similar might happen to him. He was asked to give statements about other monks, which the Secret Police would then use as evidence to imprison them. Macarius replied, "My beloved, I did not become a monk to serve as a traitor, but to perfect my life through prayer, imitating my predecessors in faith."

The police officer promised that if he complied he would be appointed bishop, a real honor. (In the Soviet Union, the atheist government decided who would lead a church.)

He replied, "Better to be a small daisy." For his steadfastness, Macarius was beaten until blood flowed from his mouth, nose, and ears, yet he remained alive.

Looking at such heroes of faith, we had to sanctify ourselves, bearing with love, joy, and humility the crosses we received. Millions are in danger of not knowing about the great and dreadful day of the Lord. What preparation does one need for this? Just readiness for sacrifice.

During the nineteenth century, when the story of West Indian slavery became known to the Moravian church, the news was that it was impossible to reach the slaves because slaveholders would not allow evangelizing. So two missionaries went to the West Indies and worked on the plantations as slaves under the lash. The slaves themselves, touched by their sacrifice, were thus prepared for "that great day."

This is the spirit that animates our mission. We unleashed a storm of prayer for Communist countries. We bombarded them with the gospel. The dissolution of the Soviet Union and the fall of the Berlin Wall represent God's answer. We give Him the glory.

~83~

THE HUMBLE GLORIFY CHRIST

AUL WAS ABLE TO WRITE, "NOR OF MEN sought we glory, neither of you, nor yet of others, when we might have been burdensome, as the apostles of Christ" (1 Thessalonians 2:6).

A Christian is supposed to be humble in his private affairs. When hit on one cheek he turns the other. The canvas never quarrels with the painter. He is free to paint on it what he likes, be it a beggar or a king. The Christian accepts any condition in life as coming from God. If he is successful, he does not boast of it. Can a brush boast that a beautiful picture has been drawn with it? Only the master painter deserves glory. So is our relationship with Christ. A Christian seeks glory from no one.

Therese of Lisieux gives a tiny illustration in her autobiography. One day while standing near a sister who was washing the laundry, she was carelessly splashed in her face with dirty water. If Therese had left suddenly without uttering a word of reproach, the sister might have guessed that she had done something wrong and been sad about it. If she had said, "Stop it!," a quarrel might have arisen.

Therese said to herself, "What is wrong with being splashed with dirty water? Jesus, the Son of God, allowed himself to 'be spat upon.'" Thinking like this, she began to like the dirt with which she was sprinkled. For you too this is the best response when subjected to humiliations in private life.

Christ was humble, as was St. Paul, though their humility had such a special feature that it was difficult to make others understand it. Jesus had to say, "I seek not mine own glory" (John 8:50), and "I am meek and lowly in heart" (Matthew 11:29). Paul also had to assure men that he sought no glory. Normally, a humble man does not go around boasting about his humility. It is only when he makes an impression of great pride, or even arrogance that he has to explain what is in him.

Don't worry if, when you humble yourself, others consider you haughty. A Christian is humble in his own affairs, yet he is very sure that he has a message from God. This he asserts with full authority, ready to contend with anyone, even to the point of being considered burdensome or annoying, or giving the impression of being an "I-know-better" man. "Apostles of Christ might be burdensome" (1 Thessalonians 2:6). Paul was such when he wrote that he sought no glory from men.

We too are unworthy messengers, but we have a worthy message. We once received a highly interesting letter from an American Christian:

> *In my neighborhood I am considered a poor man, because my income is low, but I am respected. Others have less than I. But I have enough even to give aid to the poor. So I am wealthy. I am also rich with chil-dren. I have twelve.*
>
> *When I read R. Wurmbrand's book,* Tortured for Christ, *I decided to do something for the persecuted Christians. So I got more copies and placed them in obvious places where they would be found. I put my name and phone in each book; so that those touched by the message might contact me for common prayer. I thought: Should I pray?*
>
> *If my house caught fire, I would not only pray for the burning to cease or for the fire department to*

> come, I would pray and call the firemen too, and I
> would get out my own fire hose. I decided to prepare
> a talk on this subject and send it to all churches,
> asking the pastors to invite me to deliver it.
>
> I will also take your books about atrocities suffered
> by Christians in Communist lands to all Christian
> bookstores and will ask them to display them well. My
> brethren who live under Communism risk imprison-
> ment and death for delivering a written message.
> Should I not risk some inconvenience?
>
> I am a man with only one year of high school and
> do hard work. I was a drunkard. A brother prayed for
> me and now I am God's child.

I recommend that you be as enthusiastic and practical as this brother in the service of the Lord, wherever He might call you.

Nowadays, people suffer from neglect, from the fact that no one converses with them. Their loved ones prefer to watch television. Knock at the doors of friends and neighbors, assure them that you don't wish to disturb their privacy but, on the contrary, wish to help them learn of communion with God by giving them the examples of those who achieved it even under bloody dictatorship. Such a program is not utopian. We rejoice now that Communism has suffered a huge defeat at our hands.

The Soviets themselves had a foreboding of what was to come. Their publishing house "Politicheskoye Izdatelstvo" issued in 1972 a book called *Subversion Without Dynamite*, by Belov and Shilkin. It showed pictures of Christian literature smuggled in, cars with special hiding places, Christian books imported disguised in covers of novels, magazines found under the carpets of trains arriving from the West, balloons flying over their territory and releasing Christian tracts, and so on. The Soviets described as "a bunch of criminals" all missions like ours. They call our books "dynamite." They were right.

84

THE SECRET OF SUCCESS

OLD TESTAMENT JOSEPH SAID, "BEHOLD, THERE come seven years of great plenty throughout all the land of Egypt" (Genesis 41:29). Why this exceptional blessing over Egypt? Why should it have great plenty and be warned of famine in meager years to follow? There are three reasons for this that are also the secrets of a successful mission:

1. *The Pharaoh of that time was every inch a king.*

   He acted as a king not only when awake. His subconscious was also filled with concern for the welfare of his people and so he dreamt about it at night. Every Christian is a king. Luther said, "A Christian is a perfectly free lord of all, subject to none." But a Christian is a loving king. Therefore, Luther adds, "A Christian is a dutiful servant of all, subject to all." A Christian does not have to strive to be a soul winner—it is no imposition to place the well-being of the Church first. His Christian belief has pervaded his subconscious. He simply is a soul winner, a man who puts God's Kingdom first. When he falls asleep, when the power of will disappears, the extension of God's Kingdom is his dream. My dream, from the first day of my conversion, was to witness for Christ to the Russians. Such dreams are always fulfilled.

2. *Pharaoh, the dreamer of good, met another dreamer of dreams, Joseph, and united with him.*

When I came to the West after many years of dreaming in Communist prisons about a mission to the Communist world, I met Western pastors and believers who had the same dream but did not know how to fulfill it. We could unite.

3. *Pharaoh was completely unprejudiced.*

He was advised to call to his court a foreigner with another color of skin, a man with what must have seemed to Pharaoh a queer religion, a man who worshiped only one unseen God, a prisoner with a very bad reputation. The charge for which he had been jailed was assault on a woman with intent to rape. But for this Pharaoh, every man was first of all a man.

Every man could be used for the welfare of the country. Men who had committed very bad deeds yesterday could have become good men this morning. And besides, who knew if the charges against Joseph were true? Slaveholders like Potiphar often jailed their slaves without a fair trial.

We too have maintained an attitude devoid of prejudice. Is a man a Communist torturer? St. Paul was also a torturer of Christians. A torturer can be a future apostle. We know no prejudice against him. We just love him and try to win him for Christ.

Is someone a traitor of the Underground Church, or is there a church leader in the West who compromises with Communism? We realize that the heart of every man is easily deceived. We love him and try to win him for the right attitude.

Communism wanted to dominate the white, black, and yellow peoples of the earth. Death and Communism, one of its harbingers, want men of all races. But so does love, and "Love is strong as death" (Song of Songs 8:6). We can love the political right-winger and left-winger, the fundamentalist or modernist, and all those in between. We can love the Khmer Rouge and the North Koreans, as well as those who oppose them. We do not admit any prejudice in our heart. We are serious when we sing, "Crown Him King of all."

The fulfilling of these conditions gave Egypt great plenty and provision for themselves and their neighbors in the days of famine. The fulfilling of these conditions also made our mission work obtain great victories, which were followed by even greater ones.

I offer you the examples of valiant men and women of our missions, along with heroes of faith in conditions of great suffering. Inspired by them, you too may lead a life of true fulfillment and usefulness for the Kingdom of God. You too may cause Him to "rejoice over you with singing" (Zephaniah 3:17).

Meet Richard Wurmbrand

*P*astor Richard Wurmbrand (1909-2001) was an evangelical minister who endured fourteen years of Communist imprisonment and torture in his homeland of Romania. Few names are better known in Romania, where he is one of the most widely recognized Christian leaders, authors, and educators.

In 1945, when the Communists seized Romania and attempted to control the churches for their purposes, Richard Wurmbrand immediately began an effective, vigorous "underground" ministry to his enslaved people as well as the invading Russian soldiers. He was arrested in 1948, along with his wife Sabina. His wife was a slave-laborer for three years on the Danube Canal. Richard Wurmbrand spent three years in solitary confinement, seeing no one but his Communist torturers. He was then transferred to a group cell, where the torture continued for five more years.

Due to his international stature as a Christian leader, diplomats of foreign embassies asked the Communist government about his safety and were informed that he had fled Romania. Secret police, posing as released fellow-prisoners, told his wife of attending his burial in the prison cemetery. His family in Romania and his friends abroad were told to forget him because he was dead.

After eight and a half years in prison, he was released and immediately resumed his work with the Underground Church. A couple of years later, in 1959, he was re-arrested and sentenced to twenty-five years in prison.

Mr. Wurmbrand was released in a general amnesty in 1964, and again continued his underground ministry. Realizing the great danger of a third imprisonment, Christians in Norway negotiated with the Communist authorities for his release from Romania. The Communist government had begun "selling" their political prisoners. The "going price" for a prisoner was $1,900; the price for Wurmbrand was $10,000.

In may 1966, he testified before the U.S. Senate's Internal Security Subcommittee and was striped to the waist to show the scars of eighteen deep torture wounds covering his torso. His story was carried across the world in newspapers throughout the U.S., Europe, and Asia. Wurmbrand was warned in September 1966 that the Communist regime of Romania planned to assassinate him; yet he was not silent in the face of this death threat.

Founder of the Christian mission, The Voice of the Martyrs, he and his wife traveled throughout the world establishing a network of over thirty offices that provide relief to the families of imprisoned Christians in Islamic nations, Communist Vietnam, China, and other countries where Christians are persecuted for their faith. His message has been, "Hate the evil systems, but love your persecutors. Love their souls, and try to win them for Christ."

Pastor Wurmbrand authored numerous books, which have been translated into over sixty languages throughout the world. Christian leaders have called him the "Voice of the Underground Church" and "the Iron Curtain Paul."

MEET SABINA WURMBRAND

*S*abina Wurmbrand (1913-2000) was the wife of Pastor Richard Wurmbrand and co-founder of The Voice of the Martyrs. Born into an Orthodox Jewish family in what is now the Ukraine, Sabina studied chemistry in Paris at the Sorbonne for two years. Following her return to Bucharest, Romania, for employment, she met her future husband and married in 1936.

Within months of their marriage, the Jewish couple met a German carpenter who placed a Bible into their hands, encouraging them to read about the most famous Jewish person, Jesus Christ. Sabina and Richard converted and were baptized, joining the church of the Anglican Mission to the Jews in Bucharest, Romania. Their only son, Mihai (Michael), was born in 1939.

During the Nazi occupation of Romania in 1940-43, Sabina's parents, two sisters, and one brother were killed in Nazi concentration camps. From 1940 to 1945, Sabina and Richard, both fluent in many languages, carried on intense, illegal missionary work. They smuggled Jewish children out of ghettos, preached in bomb shelters, and were arrested several times for underground Christian activated during a state of war. Sabina and her husband were spared from execution through the intervention of the chief editor of Romania's main newspaper and interest shown in their case by prominent religious leaders.

Shortly after the end of WWII, Sabina traveled to Budapest on the roof of a train filled with Russian soldiers, to smuggle in goods and food that were needed by refugees living in Hungary. With a million Russian soldiers invading Romania, Sabina and Richard's missionary activities only increased. They had not only hidden Jews in their home from the Nazis during the war, but loved their enemies by hiding Germans immediately after WWII when they were hunted on the streets like cattle by Russian troops.

As the communists attempted to control the churches for their own purposes, Richard and Sabina launched their underground ministry to enslaved Romanians as well as the occupying Russian forces. Secretly the Wurmbrands published one million Russian Gospels, along with 100,000 books that were eventually distributed in cafes, parks, railway stations, anywhere Russian soldiers were found.

Two religious summer camps attended by hundreds of Romania's religious personalities were organized in 1946 and 1947 in the Romanian mountains where Sabina led daily devotions. She also conducted street meetings with gatherings of over 5,000 people. Sabina, an excellent speaker in her own right, was instrumental in the formation of a 1,000-member Jewish-Christian church in Bucharest.

So effective was their work that Richard was arrested by the Communist government in 1948. Upon his arrest, Sabina began encouraging young ministers throughout the country to continue their underground activities.

Sabina was also arrested in 1951 and spent three years in Romanian slave-labor camps and prisons. During her captivity, she was a tireless witness as she testified of her faith and encouraged fellow prisoners.

In 1966, following Richard's release, the family escaped Romania. For the remaining 32 years of her life, Sabina traveled throughout most of the countries of the free world, speaking at meetings as the couple built the foundation of their newly founded mission to the persecuted Church, The Voice of the Martyrs.

THE PERSECUTED CHURCH

The Voice of the Martyrs has many books, videos, brochures, and other products to help you learn more about the persecuted Church. In the U.S., to request a resource catalog, order materials, or receive our free monthly newsletter, call (800) 747-0085 or write to:

The Voice of the Martyrs
PO Box 443
Bartlesville, OK 74005
USA
E-Mail: thevoice@persecution.com
Web Site: http://wwwpersecution.com

If you are in Canada, England, Australia, New Zealand, or South Africa, contact:

Australia
The Voice of the Martyrs
PO Box 598
Penrith NSW 2751
Australia
Email: thevoice@persecution.com.au
Website: www.persecution.com.au

Canada

The Voice of the Martyrs
PO Box 117
Port Credit
Mississauga, Ontario L5G 4L5
Canada
Email: thevoice@persecution.net
Website: www.persecution.net

New Zealand

The Voice of the Martyrs
PO Box 69-158
Glendene, Auckland 1230
New Zealand
Email: thevoice@persecution.co.nz
Website: www.persecution.co.nz

South Africa

Christian Mission International
P.O. Box 7157
1417 Primrose Hill
South Africa
Email: cmi@icon.co.za

United Kingdom

Release International
P.O. Box 54
Orpington BR5 9RT
United Kingdom
Website: www.releaseinternational.org
Email: infor@releaseinternational.org

INDEX OF NAMES AND PLACES

B

C

H

I

J

105, 107-108, 114, 118, 122, 129-130, 132, 135, 137, 144-145, 148, 152-153, 157, 166-167, 170-172, 177-178, 186-187, 190-191, 195, 199-203, 220, 228, 231, 233, 240-242, 246-247, 252-253, 259-260, 264-265, 268-269, 271-273, 275, 281-282

Jilava 121
Judith 239
Jue, John Han Ding 193-194

K

Kaldy 76
Karev, Baptist Pastor 91
Kasimov 207
Kasparovitch 27-28
Katona 76
Kaunas 128
Kempner, Klaus 268
Kengir 50
Kenya 263
Khmer Rouge 287
Khoury, Mary 187
Khrushchev 155
Kiangsi, Red China 183
Kishinev 13
Kislovodsk 171
Kiwanuka, Joseph 263
Klassen 81, 177, 221
Klassen, David 221
Knoerl, Killian 144
Kokhlov, Nikolai 255
Kolbe, Maximilian 145
Komsomol, the Communist Youth Organization 210
Konnikov, I., KGB officer 214
Koran [holy book of the Muslims] 210
Kosygin 132, 155, 246
Kosygin, Mrs 246
Kotchurov, John 45

RICHARD WURMBRAND

Marshall, Bishop 76
Martinson, Brother 256
Marx and Satan 266
Mary X 72, 74, 76
Mary, Sister L 173
Matchalov 207
Matveeva, Matrena 167
Medvedev, Roy 75
Micaela 159
Michelangelo 107
Mihai 239
Mihail, Father 89-90
Miller, Maskey 276
Milot 222
Moiseev, Nikolai 137
Moiseev, Vanya 53
Moldovanu 145
Molodioj Gruzii 207
Molodioj Moldavii 208
Molokani 214
Moravian Church 278
Morescat, General 33
Morse, George 41
Morse, Samuel 41
Moscow 86, 92, 136, 140, 171-172, 266
Mozambique 239
Museum of Atheism 170
Muslim 143, 166, 187, 258, 260
Myanmar 143

N
Napoleon 23, 33
Nasaruk, Valerii 227
Nauka I Religia, 171, 213, 266
Neditch, Vidal 65
Neffrim, Testsray 263
Nikiforov-Voighin   *****

U

V

W

X

Y

Z